Rural Livelihood Development in Tripura

An MGNREGS Experience

Rural Livelihood Development in Tripura

An MGNREGS Experience

Prof. Debarshi Mukherjee

Head, Department of Business Management,
Tripura University, India

Dr. Rajesh Chatterjee

Assistant Professor, Centre for the Study of Social Exclusion and Inclusive Policy, Tripura University, India

Sudakhina Mitra

Research Scholar, Department of Business Management,
Tripura University, India

Kaveri Books

New Delhi - 110002

Rural Livelihood Development in Tripura: An MGNREGS Experience

by Prof. Debarshi Mukherjee, Dr. Rajesh Chatterjee, Ms. Sudakhina Mitra

Sponsored by:
Indian Council for Social Science Research (ICSSR), New Delhi

Scheme:
Impactful Policy Research in Social Science (IMPRESS), New Delhi

First Published in 2022

ISBN: 978-81-955493-0-6

Published by

Kaveri Books

4832/24, Ansari Road, Darya Ganj
New Delhi - 110 002 (India)
Tel.: 011-2328 8140, 47072321
E-mail: kaveribooks@gmail.com
web: www.kaveribooks.com

Typeset by: Aarati Computers, New Delhi

PRINTED IN INDIA

Biplab Kumar Deb

CHIEF MINISTER OF TRIPURA
AGARTALA - 799010

Foreword

I feel immensely pleased to write the foreword for the book titled Rural Livelihood Development of Tripura: An MGNRES Experience published by Kaveri Books, New Delhi, jointly authored by Prof. Debarshi Mukherjee and Dr. Rajesh Chatterjee, the teachers of Tripura University and Ms. Sudakhina Mitra, a research scholar of the Department of Business Management, Tripura University. It is also heartening to know that the book is an outcome of a two-year long research project funded by the Indian Council of Social Science Research (ICSSR), New Delhi, under its Impactful Policy Research Scheme (IMPRESS).

While glancing through the pages, I found this book is a product of evidence-based research work that captures the data from the field drawn from each district of the state. The book elaborates the impact of MGNREGS activities in enhancing rural livelihood in Tripura and also compares the spread of such activities with the North-Eastern states. Future researchers in the same domain may seek definite guidance from the study findings for policymaking and academic discourse. I have no hesitation in stating that the book is highly contextual and in tune with the demand of time and space. I hope this book will address the pressing concerns of the rural livelihood, wage employment, economic development, growth of employment, and social justice. I am quite confident; this book would also provide further impetus to more incisive research work in relevant areas of national flagship programmes like PMEGP, Mahatma Gandhi National Rural Employment Scheme, etc.

I congratulate the authors and members of the research team who had painstakingly trudged through this difficult time and braved the fear of COVID - 19 pandemic to complete the study.

I send them warm greetings and wish them success in all future endeavours.

(Biplab Kumar Deb)

Office: Room No. 1312, New Capital Complex, Agartala - 799010, Tripura
Phone: 0381-2414000, 2414003, 2414318, Fax: 2413201, e-mail: cmoffice-tr@gov.in

प्रो. गंगा प्रसाद प्रसाईं
कुलपति
Prof. Ganga Prasad Prasain
Vice-Chancellor

त्रिपुरा विश्वविद्यालय
(केन्द्रीय विश्वविद्यालय)
सूर्यमणिनगर-799022, त्रिपुरा, भारत
Tripura University
(A Central University)
Suryamaninagar-799022, Tripura, India

Foreword

I have great pleasure in reading the book titled Rural Livelihood Development in Tripura: An Mahatma Gandhi National Rural Employment Guarantee Scheme (MGNREGS) Experience. The book highlights some vital issues critical for the state of Tripura in the functioning of the MGNREGS towards securing livelihood for its people.

The MGNREGS scheme has received unprecedented attention from researchers, much of it under the aegis of the central Ministry of Rural Development. However, there is not much evidence of research targeting the livelihood aspect of the programme under any state-specific situation. There is indeed a need for well-evidenced research on the MGNREGS and rural livelihood, and this book is a welcome addition to the literature.

In my view, this book makes a significant contribution to the scholarship on the MGNREGS. I believe this book will drive inclusive research towards development programmes focusing on livelihood generation implemented in the state and the country.

I appreciate the effort of the authors and the research team for their sincere and meticulous effort in bringing up this evidence based research captured nicely in the book. I wish them success and encourage them to advance with a similar and good piece of work in the future.

(Prof. Ganga Prasad Prasain)

प्रोफेसर राजीव मोहन पंत
कुलपति
Prof. Rajive Mohan Pant
Vice-Chancellor

असम विश्वविद्यालय
(एक केन्द्रीय विश्वविद्यालय)
सिलचर 788011 असम, भारत
ASSAM UNIVERSITY
(A Central University)
Silchar 788011, Assam, India

Foreward

I feel privileged and honored to present this book for the convenience of development functionaries, especially in the field of livelihood development of the rural community. It is an attempt to present the Mahatma Gandhi National Rural Employment Guarantee Scheme (MGNREGS) and its initiatives for livelihood development in an attractive and pleasant format so that the Government and Rural Development Practitioners can take the necessary steps to formulate a comprehensive developmental plan to provide required facilities to the Blocks/ Panchayats /Villages in strengthening the mandate further. I have known the authors personally, and I can vouch for their sincere efforts in bringing out this book titled '***Rural Livelihood Development in Tripura– An MGNREGS Experience***' published by Kaveri Books, New Delhi.

This book also serves as practical guide for the beneficiaries who can easily understand and capitalize on improving their livelihood besides achieving sustained development and economic growth.

Rural development is crucial for transforming India, and Tripura also needs strong rural development interventions. Tripura is no exception, as its economy largely depends upon the agricultural sector. Realizing the importance of the agrarian economy, this book shall serve as a periodical for the rural population of Tripura on MGNREGS experience in the State. It will make the community aware of the programme's various aspects, conditions, and scope.

I congratulate the authors Debarshi, Rajesh & Sudakhina for the efforts they have put in bringing out this book and hope that they will strive to keep close coordination with the masses with relevant publications in the future.

5.04.2022

(Prof. R.M Pant)
Vice-Chancellor
Assam University, Silchar

Phone: +91 3842 270801 (Office) Fax: +91 3842 270802 (Office), Cell + 9194350 73676, E-mail vc@aus.ac.in

Acknowledgements

1. District Magistrates and Collectors of all Districts
2. Block Development Officers (BDO) of all Blocks
3. All members of Zilla Parishads and Panchayat Samitis of all Districts
4. All Gram Pradhans of all Panchayats
5. All members of Gram Panchayats
6. All Secretaries of Gram Panchayats
7. District Magistrates for coordinating with the BDOs at the Block level for collection of meso level data.
8. All Block Development Officers for coordinating meetings with the panchayat members at the Block Level.
9. Gram Pradhans, Members and Secretaries of Gram Panchayats, Members of Zilla Parishads and Panchayat Samitis for their contribution of and inputs in the collection of data from meso level and micro level.
10. Different Departments in the Government of Tripura for providing valuable inputs. Directorate of Panchayats, Planning Department, Directorate of Economics and Statistics, Government of Tripura for sharing development statistics of the State.
11. Research Assistants Field Investigators, Data tabulators for their valuable help in the field for data collection, data entry and tabulation.

Executive Summary

Since 1952, there were several programmes like National Rural Employment Programme (NREP), Rural Landless Employment Guarantee Programme (RLEGP), Jawahar Rozgar Yojona (JRY) and Sampoorna Gramin Rozgar Yojona (SGRY) were undertaken by the Government of India to eradicate poverty in accelerating the rural economy. The main focus was on absorption of under-employment and to provide supplementary wage employment to the rural poor. But gross unjustness was found in rural livelihood. So, there was a high demand and need to ensure a certain minimum days of employment to the rural people and hence National Rural Employment Guarantee Act (NREGA) was enacted on September, 2005 by the Parliament of India, which is known as Mahatma Gandhi National Rural Employment Guarantee Act (MGNREGA).

The Mahatma Gandhi National Rural Employment Guarantee Scheme (MGNRES) was launched on February, 2006 under the mandate of MGNREGA-2005, to enhance livelihood security of the households in rural areas and to engage the adult rural members in the unskilled manual work.

The main objective of Mahatma Gandhi National Rural Employment Guarantee Scheme (MGNREGS) is to provide a right-based 100 days of unskilled employment for enhancing the rural poor's purchasing power and capacity to overcome hunger and poverty. However, this objective has not been achieved in any state so far at the aggregate level. The MGNREG scheme has high expectations regarding employment generation, alleviation of poverty, food security, halting migration, and overall rural development. However, since the beginning of the MGNREGA implementation project, no such study has been undertaken for

Tripura, where a sincere effort has been made to measure whether their participation in the project has benefited the livelihood of rural people.

With retrospective approaches over the decades on the poverty alleviation and infrastructure development programmes, the Government of India shaped its vast employment opportunity for the unskilled masses with the name of National Rural Employment Guarantee Act (NREGA) in 2005, later known as Mahatma Gandhi National Rural Employment Guarantee Act (MGNREGA). Since its inception, MGNREGA has been contributing in the areas of asset creation through generating employment, social justice, empowerment, infrastructural development, health care, governance, and many other aligned sectors for the rural population. Through a decade of success in transforming rural livelihood, the Government of India is planning to increase the man-days and stretch it towards the urban sector unskilled masses. The process of designing the present and future well-being of the economy and environment – the two vital elements of human development is called Sustainable Development, and that is what Mahatma Gandhi National Rural Employment Guarantee Act (MGNREGA) aims for. Though the focus of the MGNREG Scheme (MGNREGS) is on augmenting wage employment but it has been working from its inception to accomplish several goals that cover most of the areas of SDGs such as natural resource management (NRM) issues and the reasons of poverty like drought, soil erosion and deforestation thereby encouraging sustainable development. The term livelihood infrastructure takes a broader role in MGNREGS rather than developing mere physical infrastructures. While the impacts of the MGNREGA as a safety net programme are well established, very little is known whether the assets created for livelihood generation under the MGNREGS have improved the standard of living of the rural poor during their participation in the programme.

Based on the review of extant literature, a research model has been developed which identifies Infrastructure Development at Macro level (Asset A & D), Administrative Monitoring & Control, Social Justice, Environment Development and Public Health Care Systems as the independent variable which impacts the Rural Livelihood Development of the rural folk participating in MGNREGS projectconsidered as the dependent variable. These independent variables have been further quantified into measurable units.

Development of rural livelihood (dependent variable) could be measured by three items which are ;

a. Income level is an essential determinant of one's economic prosperity and has a bearing on ones's livelihood.
b. Asset (B & D) which could be measured by land productivity, horticulture, sericulture, fisheries and agricultural production.
c. Socialstatus could be measured by family education, social awareness and community relationship.

Based on the above model, the study develops five hypotheses, revealing the independent variables' impact on the dependent variable.

A Z-score test has been applied on government data related to MGNREGS collected from various government offices through elected members/functionaries to identify sample blocks and villages at the macro level. The authors used a random sampling method with a vigil for such areas to provide recommendations at the State and Central levels. The impact of the MGNREGS on the Most Developed Panchayat (MDP) and Less Developed Panchayat (LDP) has been found by collecting primary data with the help of a pre-framed questionnaire and adopting Focus Group Discussion, Semi-Structured Interview (SSI), and In-depth Interview.

It was found that IV3, i.e., Social Justice is the most critical predictor (62%) while IV2, i.e., Administrative Monitoring & Control (18%) and Environment Development (12.9%) are the second and third important predictors. Therefore, it could be concluded that MGNREGS is working steadfastly not only in rural livelihood development but also as a powerful instrument in providing social justice to the rural people andthe development of the overall environment.

The Public Health Care System at the ground level across all eight districts of Tripura needs significant up-gradation as the people at the bottom of the pyramid need healthcare facilities, particularly in remote areas. This finding is in sync with the NITI Aayog's report of 2019, wherein Tripura is placed at the moderately improved state in terms of incremental performance in health care services among the smaller states of India. The main objective of MGNERGS is to create assets at the community and individual levels.However, the study finds a lacuna in the formation of assets at these levels as it contributes merely 6.2% in the predictor's importance table, thus causing a negative impact on livelihood development. The finding corroborates Tripura's rank at the national level in creating jobs (ranked at 8th position with unemployment rate 20% as of May 2021).

Development of roads, improvement of availability of drinking water, improvement in sanitation system and sanitation facilities, improvement of irrigation system, improvement of water conservation activities like restoration of water bodies, rainwater conservation etc., improvement of watershed management are suggested where the policymakers must concentrate to realize the underlying objective of the MGNREGS.

Further, it is also recommended that the health care facilities should be fostered to provide the best services to the rural poor. Some specific improvements viz. increase in the number of public health centers, Doctors in PHCs and CHCs, improvement of family hygiene, increase in the number of nursing staff and other health staff in PHCs and CHC, increase in the number of medical shops, availability of medicines in local hospitals, availability of minimum clinical test facility in local hospitals may be brought under the purview of MGNREGS works which may contribute to the improvement of overall health condition of the household.

Preface

Since 1952, there were several programmes like National Rural Employment Programme (NREP), Rural Landless Employment Guarantee Programme (RLEGP), Jawahar Rozgar Yojona (JRY) and Sampoorna Gramin Rozgar Yojona (SGRY) were undertaken by the Government of India to eradicate poverty in accelerating the rural economy. The main focus was on absorption of under-employment and to provide supplementary wage employment to the rural poor. But gross unjustness was found in the implementation of rural livelihood programmes. So, there was a high demand and need to ensure a certain minimum days of employment to the rural people and hence National Rural Employment Guarantee Act (NREGA) was enacted on September, 2005 by the Parliament of India, which is known as Mahatma Gandhi National Rural Employment Guarantee Act (MGNREGA).

The Mahatma Gandhi National Rural Employment Guarantee Scheme (MGNRES) was launched on February, 2006 under the mandate of MGNREGA-2005, to enhance livelihood security of the households in rural areas and to engage the adult rural members in the unskilled manual work.

15-4-2022
Agartala, Tripura

Prof. Debarshi Mukherjee
Dr. Rajesh Chatterjee
Sudakhina Mitra

Contents

List of Tables

List of Figure

1

Introduction to Mahatma Gandhi National Rural Employment Guarantee Scheme (MGNREGS)

The 11th Five-Year Plan of India reiterated inclusive growth and development as socio-economic targets committed by the MDG's which include reducing the headcount poverty ratio, creating new job opportunities, and increasing the wage rate (http://nrega.nic.in/call paper.pdf). Therefore to address poverty and related issues, the Union Government evolved with a wage employment programme called the National Rural Employment Guarantee Act (NREGA) in 2005, later renamed as Mahatma Gandhi National Rural Employment Guarantee Act (MGNREGA) with a pattern shift not only focusing on providing basic facilities for a living but also on inclusive growth, natural resource management, productive assets creation, environment development, rural women empowerment and rural-urban migration with the multiple objectives of sustaining income and consumption through wage works, creating durable assets (Rhonda Breitkreuz, et. al., 2017).

Like other developing nations, India had comprehensively focused on limiting extreme poverty and hunger towards combating chronic diseases while achieving a universal primary education with a global partnership for inclusive development. The Sustainable Development Goals (SDG) or Global Goals were framed in 2015 with 17 specific targets for better inclusive growth of all. With the initiation of a robust approach from the exclusive MDG's towards the inclusive SDGs, the core goal remained on the complete eradication of extreme poverty and providing food security with sustained economic growth for building productive employment opportunities and building resilient infrastructure (sustainabledevelopment.un.org).

With a dedicated vigil to escalate the growth and development of the rural sectors, MGNREGA has been contributing to asset creation through generating employment, social justice, empowerment, infrastructural development, health care, governance and many others aligned sectors for the rural population. Through a decade of success in transforming rural livelihood, the Government of India is planning to increase the man-days and stretch it towards the urban sector unskilled masses.

Sustainable Development Goals (SDGs) of 2030 are set to design a beautiful future for the world. Though the focus of the MGNREG Scheme (MGNREGS) is on augmenting wage employment, since inception, it has been working to accomplish several goals that cover most of the areas of SDGs such as natural resource management (NRM), issues and the reasons of poverty like drought, soil erosion and deforestation thereby encouraging sustainable development.

The term livelihood infrastructure takes a broader role in MGNREGS rather than physical infrastructure. The benefits of MGNREGA are well established, but whether the assets created for livelihood generation under the MGNREGS have been able to upgrade the living standards of the rural poor while their participation in the programme is yet to be explored. During 2012-

2013, the number of work-days provided, on an average to the rural households was 86%; Tripura topped in this and continued the position for the next three years. The primary reasons behind the success were the absence of employment-oriented government programmes, proper administrative monitoring and control, technology use in the management of the programme at the Block and District level.

To sustain with the same vigor and relevance, the program's approach needs to be revised. At this time, the qualitative aspect of the programme needs heavy emphasis. In terms of quantity, MGNREGS has already contributed to the rural areas with livelihood assets and infrastructure; now, for taking up further asset creation, a need assessment should be there at the community level, keeping in mind the available resources so that funds are not wasted. The new-fangled needs of the people can be adjusted accordingly. Apart from its direct benefits to households, the programme is also expected to add a quality aspect to life: the extent to which an individual can avail essential possibilities of life.

1.1. MGNREGS in the North Eastern Region and Tripura

Since independence, economic problems have posed a severe challenge for North-East India and Tripura is no exception. Due to inadequate Central Government aid and investment in the infrastructural facilities and failure in the past to exploit the natural resources, the state failed to develop to the desirable extent leading to growing unemployment and resentment among the youth (Debnath and Neogi, 2013). Thus, MGNREGS becomes highly critical in the state. In the first stage, the scheme was first introduced in Dhalai District, followed by West Tripura and South Tripura in the second stage, and in the North Tripura district during the third stage when the programme was made universal across the country.

The proportion of employment seekers among job-card holders and in terms of person-days generated, the State ranks highest followed by Nagaland, Mizoram and Manipur, and many other large states. It has created more than 3439 lakhs of workdays for its people over 2016-2020 (Bhowmik, 2013).

Though priority is given to generating employment, in terms of creating physical assets and in terms of an absolute number of works taken up among the North-Eastern states, Tripura tops, which is even higher than many other bigger states in India (Bhowmik, 2013).

An upliftment in the life and livelihood of the participating poor households in the North-Eastern region can be possible only if the key objectives of the scheme like average person-days generated, complete 100 days of work, and the work completion rate is fulfilled. (Bhowmik & Bose, 2015).

Table-1: Output Indicators of North Eastern Indian States (2018-2019 & 2019-2020)

States	Average Person Days/ HH		HHs with 100 days		Work Completion rate	
	2018-2019	2019-2020	2018-2019	2019-2020	2018-2019	2019-2020
Arunachal Pradesh	1572.6	1569.4	412	292	68.42	41.71
Assam	1179.13	1221.2	18360	30052	75.71	35.77
Manipur	731.06	1228.2	16	857	85.67	76.23
Meghalaya	1838.63	1801.01	160908	180536	78.28	41.91
Mizoram	814.12	873.08	81736	157672	99.52	96.89
Nagaland	766.47	869.56	0	1	81.54	41.93
Sikkim	1520.9	1489.9	4668	3550	72.34	40.75
Tripura	989.9	1152.99	14982	55381	99.33	90.65

Source : Calculated from www.mgnrega.nic.in

Considering the output indicators, Table-1 indicates a higher average person-days per household. In 2018-19 & 2019-20, the state was the second-best performer in the North-Eastern region after Mizoram in terms of work completion rate in the country. However, Tripura was trailing behind the national average with respect to providing 100 days of work.

Coming to the asset development criteria of the programme that relate to SDGs such as natural resource management, the following table 2 shows the position of the State in comparison to other North-Eastern states.

Table-2 indicates Tripura's overall performance in NRM-related works viz., soil and water conservation, groundwater recharge, irrigation, plantation, and land-related work for livelihood support. The position of the State is much higher than any other state in North-Eastern India. Initiatives for livelihood support through land-related works during 2018-2019 and 2019-2020 in the State have increased manifolds, and it is four

Table-2: Natural Resource Management (NRM) Related Works Completed till 19-20 in the North Eastern States

Sl. No.	States	Soil and Water Conservation Related Works (32)	Ground Water Recharge Related Works (7)	Irrigation Related Works (19)	Drainage and other Related Works (16)	Plantation Related Works (17)	Land related Works for Livelihood support (9)	Total	Farm Ponds
1	2	3	4	5	6	7	8	9=3+4+5+6+7+8	10 (out of column 5)
1	ARUNACHAL PRADESH	285	11	376	72	348	64	1156	69
2	ASSAM	4907	59	5969	446	11516	2425	25322	2601
4	MANIPUR	489	63	551	321	1056	377	2857	81
5	MEGHALAYA	1301	256	952	274	3967	698	7448	174
6	MIZORAM	1435	218	1671	116	911	2713	7064	1287
7	NAGALAND	406	205	410	106	1530	299	2956	185
8	SIKKIM	402	128	193	72	1150	735	2680	1
9	TRIPURA	5976	849	18232	212	12209	8771	46249	3011
	Total	**15201**	**1789**	**28354**	**1619**	**32687**	**16082**	**95732**	**7409**

Source: Calculated from www.mgnrega.nic.in.

times higher than the state of Assam. This development also substantiates that Tripura being a landlocked state, employment opportunities and scope of development works are relatively lesser compared to other states; hence the dependence on such government programmes is very high and significant.

There is 591 village panchayats, with 901 villages in Tripura constituting about 27,12,464 lakh people, i.e.75% of the State's total population (India Village Directory, 2020). Thus, MGNREGA directly intervenes in the life and livelihood of 75% of the population, which is very rare in other parts of the country where the programme impacts approximately 30-35% of the population (www.ecostat.gov.in).

However, good in quantity gaps exist in several areas that impact service delivery, starting from understanding the programme – its positive actions, gender bias criteria inbuilt into the scheme upto the management of the programme (Pellisery & Jalan, 2011). To continue with the same relevance, the gap between quantity and quality should be bridged. It is high time to assess whether the assets built up for livelihood support of the rural population can take care of the unmet demands and how they vary across the State (Kumar et. al., 2016). Thus, the basic needs of the rural folks from the livelihood resource base should be identified first, and then the need should be adjusted with the stock of livelihood assets. Thus, rural infrastructure development in the state yields a good position but whether the need for such livelihood resources is compensated with the stock of livelihood assets created remains to be explored. This mapping can address the quality aspect of the programme and become a meaningful argument before funding the future MGNREGA projects.

Tripura being a landlocked state, employment opportunities are relatively less compared to other states; hence, dependence on such government initiatives is of paramount importance. Since the inception of the MGNREGS, no study has been undertaken for Tripura where a sincere effort has been made to measure whether the participation of the rural folks in asset development through the project has benefited the livelihood of rural people or not. Thus, the present study aims to cast light on the project's impact on developing rural livelihood, which will be a milestone in times to come. Hence, an extensive literature review was conducted to understand the veracity of the critical variables functioning within the scheme.

2

Appraisal of MGNREGS and its Potential

Mahatma Gandhi National Rural Employment Guarantee Scheme (MGNREGS) has been functioning covering the whole of rural India. As a result, it is the first heavy budget programme against other social welfare programmes of the past (Vasanthi, 2017). The programme has responded to the wage employment demand of the rural masses. Some of the important works of literature on its implementation and operational details are discussed here.

Ineffective targeting, leakages in work processes and poor quality asset creation, etc. have been the widespread problem of the wage employment programmes in the past (Aiyar and Samji, 2006). Therefore, to improve the effectiveness of the MGNREGA was approved by the Parliament on September 2005, the social

audit process was prescribed as an inbuilt mechanism within the programme.

Various loopholes were identified in the programme implementation during a review conducted by the Comptroller and Auditor General of India during 2008 (CAG, 2008). The study reported the non-availability of proper records on jobs demanded by households. Jobs were allocated verbally without documentation. Despite submitting applications, some families were not registered.

In a budgetary appraisal of MGNREGA, it was found that the institutional arrangements in weaker states were not adequate to implement the programme effectively. (Chakraborty 2007). Similarly, in the villages of Rajasthan and Andhra Pradesh, monitoring the programme implementation was done using a community control mechanism (Afridi, 2008). The study also emphasized that social audits without the support of NGOs/ CSOs is wishful thinking. Dreze et. al. (2008) found MGNREGA functioning far better in Chhattisgarh than other employment programmes. From time and again, some common hindrances like lack of trained professionals, understaffing and delay in administration, lack of people's planning, poor quality of works and assets created, inappropriate schedules have been affecting the implementation process (Ambasta et. al., 2008).

Khera (2008) observed that the farmer's organization was very effective in making MGNREGA perform better. The participation of the women workers varied mainly across the selected study areas in various states (Khera and Nayak, 2009). Kareemulla et. al., 2010 studied that works like soil and water conservation structures and construction of rural roads were taken up. The investments yield results the quality and maintenance of assets need to be attended carefully. They concluded asset creation is generally seen as a by-product in the study areas. Concerning wages, Adhikari and Bhatia, 2010 stated that direct transfer of wages into a worker's bank account was significant protection against corruption and misappropriation. Using 2009-10 NSS data, Liu and Barrett (2013) analyzed job-seeking patterns, rationing, and participation in the MGNREGA.

Anderson et. al. (2013) highlighted the significance of Unique Identification (UID) in the functioning of MGNREGA for bringing in better efficiency in its functioning. They suggested further improvement of the programme processes through the UID system through control group methodology.

According to Rawls (1971), inequalities in society result from unequal access to resources, and therefore there is a need for social justice. Social justice in the domestic sphere in countries like India is related to correcting past socio-economic and political discrimination against certain sections (SC/STs, women, religious minorities, and poor) of society who have been excluded from the mainstream development of society. Their indicators of development are abysmal, and there are even region-wise disparities. Therefore, the seventeen Sustainable Development Goals (SDGs) are set to work globally to reduce these inequalities and design a beautiful future for the world. In India, MGNREGA works to accomplish 17 Global Goals: poverty alleviation, zero hunger, health and well-being, quality education, clean water and sanitation, social justice, partnership, etc. of Sustainable Development in Rural Areas (Praveen and Margain, 2019).

In another study, Chinnaswammy (2019) measured the implication of MGNREGA in the study area of Mobiripatty Panchayat in Tamil Nadu. The findings show that the location covers large women entities with a general quota, and they are pretty satisfied with the implications of work provided by the MGNREGA. A study on identifying the development strata through satellite imaging on the areas of Nellimarla Village, Vizianagram District of Andhra Pradesh emphasizes the development of the village through achieving the SDGs and the impact of MGNREGA in the area. The satellite images of the terrain show a massive change in the measurements from 2008 until 2016. The study concludes with achieving a positive impact on gaining sustainable development on the natural resources and it appraises the growth in the assets leading to the all-round development of the population residing in the village (Dandabathula, Reddy, Mohapatra and Rao, 2019).

Midstream Marketing & Research Institute, New Delhi (2017) suggests that along with the huge investments to create assets at the village level, there is a need to make a "maintenance fund" from the allocated amount for regulation and upkeep of the asset, in the long run, will take care of the sustainable aspect of the created assets. The study reveals irregular and weak MIS networks due to slow internet connectivity. The same reason affected the geo-tagging system. The study also shows the purchasing power among the rural households, which creates demand for commodities, which again made the demand for capital, raw material and workers. Such demand multiplies the effect neglected for the increased investment of livestock and quality of education and health in rural areas, thus stimulating rural economy.

While discussing the impact of MGNREGS on income, asset creation, and food security, Mishra, Vishwanathan and Bhattarai, 2014 find that though the number of days was below 40 per annum. The wage rate was much below than the agriculture labour wage rate. Still, as the programme generally took place during the non-agricultural season, it had produced a tremendous impact on the financial stability of participating households. The programme has also solved the unavailability of other kinds of work in the villages, especially during the non-agricultural season. The beneficiaries spent the additional wage-earning to support household's food, non-food expenditures viz. educational fees, medicines, food items, purchase of buffaloes. Thus, the programme helped improve the quality of life and living standards for the future rural generation. At the same time, the collective measures at the community level to sustain the community assets were emphasized (Keerthi et. al., 2014).

On durability of assets, Pandey (2017) stated that the maintenance of assets is a permissible work under the programme which needs to be explored so that the investments do not go futile. Such exposure to asset maintenance would render a sense of belongingness and ownership. Convergence was also prescribed to ensure the durability of the assets.

In their study, Narayanan, Das, and Kulkarni (2014) attempted to examine the presence of assets and bring out the user perception of the problems and benefits associated with the work and projects. They realized that there is a substantial scope to improve the design of assets when a more inclusive work selection process is adopted. The impact of asset creation directly or indirectly benefitted the most vulnerable families by increasing their income by firm practices and wage earnings. This improved situation has led to a gradual reduction in distress migration (Sebastian, 2015).

Hanbal and Prakash (2019) focused on the discrepancies while maintaining Open Government Data linked to MGNREGA. The authors conducted semi-structured interviews and Focused Group Discussions (FGD) to identify certain issues related to the maintenance of programme data. The study prioritized the matter of data uploading by both ends of functioning, i.e. the officials and the beneficiaries. They proposed the need of adding such portals linked with the other domains of the government programmes.

Varshney (2015) observed that deployment of female labourer use is more in Rajasthan than in Uttar Pradesh. The study suggested merging the technically upgraded crop production with the labour use so that these states can generate more extensive production and more employment.

Sahoo (2014) observed a positive impact of MGNREGA in women's lives. Starting from enhancing their economic independence to boosting their self-confidence, the programme has a multiplier effect on women's life. The programme also assured minimum financial security to the rural sector, especially women and the overall economic development of the rural areas (Abhymon, Cherian, and Baba, 2018). The programme has also provided decision-making power to women in the male-dominated rural agrarian society (Xavier's and Mary, 2014). However, some critical consequences like the risk of MGNREGS fatigue, equality-based rights to manage productive assets, gender inclusion must be addressed urgently. Kelkar (2011) discusses the confidence and capability the programme has given women to change their power relations with men. To bring in gender-responsive implementation of guaranteed employment through SHGs, and Mahila Mandals. Gender Responsive Panchayat, community based organizations can be efficient models at the local level.

Dasgupta and Sudarshan (2011) provide evidence that the gender gap was primarily responsible for the worker's shift from agriculture to MGNREGA. However, Zimmerman (2012) finds that a limited impact of MGNREGA on the labour market for men. The study suggests the most critical contribution of MGNREGA has been indirect enforcement of minimum wages in the private sector during agriculture in the primary season.

In a review from West Bengal, Sultana and Rao (2016) state how MGNREGS innovatively empowered women, particularly the socially and economically backward groups. There is a significant change rate between the total individual and household workers in the state as in the rest of the country. Community skills like communication mobility, participation, and decision-making among women have tremendously increased, generating more GDP for the districts.

As a right-based and demand-based approach, the programme has acted as a tool for empowerment to the victims of social exclusion and politically marginalized by creating employment opportunities and raising wage rates within the legitimate framework of governance (Alam & Alam, 2014). The PRI bodies are strengthened and assigned significant roles to reach the most vulnerable classes and civil society groups. The primary goal is to ensure actual participation in making critical decisions that empower people and give a sense of ownership to the programme

(Singh, 2015). Thus, to strengthen public accountability, the programme envisages Social Audit to monitor the work processes despite a well-defined institutional structure to grievance redressal (Aiyar, 2011). However, studies have shown that inappropriate reporting was the major impediment to proper enforcement of Social Audit findings.

Coming to the environmental part of the programme, Tewari (2011) explains that the programme can enhance environmental services such as water for irrigation and the improvement of soil quality. For the generation of employment in ecological goods and services, proper regulation and management of the natural systems at the community levels, a prerequisite for environmental equity, needs to be prioritized (Reddy, 2012). The programme activities have reduced the vulnerability of agricultural production, water resources, and livelihoods to uncertain rainfall, water scarcity and poor soil fertilization (Esteves, 2013).

The impact of MGNREGS on migration issues has been cited differently in different works of literature. Kumar and Deogharia (2017) find that as the period for obtaining job card delays work wage and wage payment time lags in getting payment, disruption in MGNREGA works evident, thus the households lack interest in MGNREGA works and fail to contribute to improving their livelihood thereby. Therefore, the migrants choose to migrate from villages for better opportunities. Thus, MGNREGA was unable to curb migration. However, Jacob (2018) finds that the program has a positive impact on control migration when effectively implemented in the case of Villupuram, Tamil Nadu. The findings suggest that the programme can improve the coordination between rural and urban areas and provide work for a minimum of 100 days during lean agriculture season through creating basic infrastructure stable income to labour and agriculture productivity from irrigation works.

A study from Assam, one of the prominent North Eastern States, pointed out that some basic amenities related to the speculation of growth within the framework of MGNREGS implementation are lacking. The programme is a boon for the Nation's socio-economic development if proper scrutiny and supervision are carried out in these thrust areas (Das, 2018).

From the review of extant literature, it is found that the development of rural livelihood rests mostly on the following variables, namely asset build-up, good governance initiatives undertaken by the administrative agencies for better implementation of the programme, social protection and social justice measures, environmental development works undertaken and rural health initiatives launched under the MGNREGS. To understand the importance of the variables and to identify the potential research gap in the earlier works of literature, a variable wise detailed analysis has been done as follows:

2.1. Research Gap Analysis

Variable 1: Infrastructure Development (Asset Build Up)

With respect to asset build up, studies focus on the role & impact of MGNREGS towards the accomplishment of 17 Global Goals of Sustainable Development in Rural Areas (Praveen & Margain, 2019). Geographical requirement of the area for the scheme implementation should not impede asset creation; only then it can be fruitful and beneficial in the upliftment of the specified area (Bhargava, 2013). So far as the impact of asset creation is concerned, MGNREGS has directly or indirectly benefitted vulnerable families by increasing income by better farm practices and wage earnings. This improved situation has reduced distress migration (Sebastian, 2015). The additional wage earning from the programme has supported the non-food expenditures in the rural households like education fees, medicines, purchase of buffaloes, etc., thereby adding to the quality of life to the future rural generation (Keerthi, Bhattarai, Kamala & Rao, 2014). Therefore, collective measures at the community level are necessary to sustain the community assets. MGNREGS has brought financial stability to the participating households in the semi arid villages during the non agricultural seasons through assets creation activities which has solved the problem of unavailability of other kinds of work in the villages (Mishra, Vishwanathan & Bhattarai, 2014). MGNREGA has significantly raised the water conservation activities creating a positive impact on the cropping pattern resulting in a shift from low-value traditional crops to short duration high value crops (Mishra, 2010). Mukherjee and Sinha, 2011 predicts that with MGNREGS, cultivating households will employ less labour, adversely affecting production. This is also evident in some areas; however, the poor would be better off. Increases in food prices due to the introduction of NREGA are also predicted in the model.

Research Gap – Studies did not vet the performance of MGNREGS with respect to asset development based on the geographical drawbacks of the rural areas, which could have been fruitful and beneficial otherwise for the up-liftment of rural areas. The studies emphasized the demand for only some specific kind of asset creation where women participation is more but does not consider other types of assets creation like flood control, irrigational works, etc. The studies did not emphasize better monitoring mechanisms at the administrative level to enhance the production value of the assets.

Variable 2 : Administrative Monitoring and Control

UNDP recognizes nine core characteristics of good governance like Participation, the Rule of Law, Transparency, Responsiveness, etc. for implementing bodies that would impact the result of the programme at a different level (Alam & Alam, 2014). The programme had positively impacted rural-urban migration when it was implemented effectively. Moreover, the programme processes improve the coordination between rural and urban areas for providing work during lean agriculture season by creating basic infrastructure, stable income to labour and agriculture productivity from irrigation works (Jacob 2008). Harisha, Nagaraj, Chandrakantha, Murthya, Chengappac and Basavarajb (2011) analyzed the relationship between the number of days worked under the programme and the contributing factors, the number of days of work was regressed on the workers' factors like age, gender, education, family size, and landholding size. In states like Jharkhand, limited impact partly stems from a misconception of labour migration – as a poverty 'problem' and as merely a product of 'push-and-pull' economic factors (Solinski, 2013). Discussing the impact of MGNREGS on migration, Kumar and Deogharia (2017) finds that people's livelihood is not very encouraging due to the fewer days of work and, as a result, low earning. Again, due to the exact reason for fewer workdays, the programme fails to stop migration.

Research Gap – Studies not focus on the challenge of whether the supply can accommodate the demand, particularly in rural areas. However, the point has been highlighted but not further explained. Limited focus is given on capacity building of Panchayati Raj functionaries and government officials on MGNREGS guidelines, processes, and provisions but most literatures have mentioned the strengthening of PRI Bodies and assigned significant roles to reach the most vulnerable classes and civil society groups. Capacity building is an essential criterion for participatory social audit, vigilance and monitoring.

Papers have described the critical areas of Good Governance for achieving MGNREGS objectives. However, the broad and long-term perspectives of good governance like proper financial management and administrative control to yield sustainable human development have been neglected.

While discussing the migration issue, the enormous secondary benefits of the Act are not highlighted. The farmers' acreage under different crops was brought down due to labour scarcity, resulting in fallow land. This issue of labour scarcity could be addressed if the 100 days of employment were confined to months when there is no harvesting or sowing activity. Such an adjustment might yield the enormous benefits the programme intends for the rural poor.

While dealing with migration as a poverty problem, the conditions of development, that is, the social and economic factors for migration were not elaborated. Papers do not appreciate the contribution of the programme towards agricultural productivity which has resulted due to improved infrastructure in Jharkhand and women empowerment that has taken place due to the lesser number of works available to them.

Variable 3 : Social Justice

Govind Kelkar (2011) in his study attempts to draw policy attention to the multifaceted inter-relationship that is the relation between gender relations, income, and productive assets. Asset ownership in terms of land, housing technology, and economic participation have occurred in favour of women as these two are components of economic empowerment (Afridi & Iverson, 2014). Haque (2011) studies the impact of social audits on MGNREGA delivery in Andhra Pradesh using unique panel data evidences higher beneficiary learning from participation in audits and audit effectiveness in detecting irregularities. The scheme has resulted in a significant increase in the market wage rate of agricultural and non-agricultural workers and supported this claim using NSSO data. Several gaps in the implementation of MGNREGS, which need to be bridged through awareness-building campaigns, capacity building of Panchayati Raj functionaries and government officials from time to time, on the work processes, affirmative action embedded into the programme and the multi-benefits of MGNREGS (Sudarshan, 2011). The gender gap is mainly responsible for workers' shift from agriculture to MGNREGS. Borah & Bordolai (2014) mentioned that MGNREGS positively impacted the income and eco-upliftment of rural women of Sonitpur District of Assam. Still, again the scheme does not guarantee 100 days job guarantee to most cardholders. The study reveals the act couldn't shine in the state of Assam. However, the employment pattern is positive among women but much less on average compared to that of the country.

Hanbal & Prakash, (2019) focused on the discrepancies while maintaining Open Government Data linked to MGNREGA. The authors carried out Semi-structured Interviews and Focused Group Discussions to identify specific issues related to the data. The authors have prioritized the matter of data uploading by both ends of functioning, i.e., the officials and the beneficiaries. They also proposed adding such portals linked with the other domains of the Government Programmes.

Research Gap – Emphasis on the role of institutional arrangement at the local level like SHGs, Mahila Mandals, Gender Responsive Panchayats, and other Women-based and Community-based Organizations (CBOs) could have better highlighted the issue of gender, income distribution, and asset creation. Gender-Responsive implementation of guaranteed employment SHGs, Mahila Mandals, Gender Responsive Panchayats, Community based Organizations can be efficient models of such institutional arrangements at the local level. There is a positive but insignificant impact of audits on employment generation and a modest decline in the leakage amount per labour-related irregularity.

Several studies on inequality and MGNREGS highlights inequality issues comparing only the male counterparts whereas the administrative, social, and demographic settings and the programme provisions are equally responsible for such inequalities. The role of the administration to remove these gaps, render proper monitoring and control over the MGNREGS activities in the State so that valuable gains do not get derailed for poor implementation are missing. The study by Hanbal & Prakash, (2019) did not specify the weak links or missing links in the implementation of MGNREGS but has prescribed solutions for improvement. The paper did not suggest internet connectivity issues and capacity building of the technical functionaries working at the Block level.

Variable 4 : Environment Development

Esteves (2013) assesses the activities undertaken under MGNREGS to explain the program's prospects to enhance environmental services, namely water for irrigation activities and maintaining soil quality. Reddy (2012) attempts to assess the employment generated in rural India's Environmental Goods and Services (EGS) activities. Sebastian and Azeez (2014) points out that for integration of biodiversity into MGNREGS, panchayat level biodiversity registers need to be prepared, supporting individuals, institutional efforts, and appropriate policies need to be formulated. The paper finds that MGNREGS has reduced the dependency on uncertain rainfall for agricultural produce. Moreover, the program has also addressed water scarcity and poor soil fertility issues.

Research Gap – Literatures on issues pertaining to the management of natural resources through MGNREGS are regularly discussed. However, proper regulation and management of the natural systems at the community levels, a prerequisite for environmental equity, has been ignored.

Variable 5 : Rural Health

Kumar and Joshi (2013) examines the changes in household food consumption and nutritional security of poor rural households and has assessed on the dietary pattern and nutritional status of the families using the data from 66th round of National Sample Survey (NSS), 2009. MGNREGS has increased the level of food consumption for cereals and non-cereals; a substantial increase in calorie intake and protein intake has also been witnessed among households Tripathi and Wadhawan (2017). Kumar and Supriya, 2011 through a socio-economic index, it was shown that the beneficiary households who were in poor socio-economic conditionshas shown a major shift especially their access to education, health care facilities have shown a major shift. MGNREGA potential may freeze the PDS operations at a certain level to ensure minimum provisioning of the basic food commodities and give greater emphasis on employment programmes to enhance the purchasing power of low-income families, which will improve the nutritional security of rural households (Devi, Balasubramanian and Kumar, 2016).

Improvement in the sanitary conditions, conditions of kitchen, toilets, cleanliness was reported. As far as housing is concerned improved conditions were reported by the beneficiaries. The shift was from mud house to cemented house with cemented floors and walls (Kaur and Randhawa, 2016).

Research Gap – While discussing the food consumption pattern among the beneficiary households, the Kumar and Joshi, 2013 pointed out that beneficiary households spent more on fuel and light, transport, clothing but less on education, healthcare and medicines. The reasons for not spending more on education and health care, which are two vital indicators of development, have not been discussed, thereby limiting the approach of the paper towards contribution to the quality of life of rural households.

2.2. Decentralized Planning and Administration

The mass scale of MGNREGS provision required the rapid development of administrative innovations to enable effective planning, budgeting and implementation to scale, including significant decentralization. A selection of the key variables developed under MGNREGS in order to accommodate mass provision and rapid implementation of the entitlement-based programme to scale were outlined above. The realization of the variables discussed involved alongside the development of an administration with a dedicated cadre of workers, a decentralized and technology driven planning approach and the implementation of a standardized documentation system. Therefore, it becomes imperative to examine the administrative monitoring and control of activities under MGNREGS by competent authorities.

Again, MGNREGS objectives included the promotion of sustainable livelihoods from the time it was enacted.

> "*The mandate of the Act is to provide not less than one hundred days of unskilled manual work as guaranteed employment in a financial year to every household in rural areas as per demand, resulting in creation of productive*

assets of prescribed quality and durability, to strengthen the livelihood resource base of the poor." (Para 4 of Schedule-I, MGNREGA).

Initially, greater emphasis was given to employment creation rather than livelihoods promotion. It was only from 2015 that the government increased its attention to creating durable quality assets, intending to promote sustainable livelihood opportunities in the rural areas (MGNREGA, 2017c). In order to achieve these twin objectives, the programme aims to create rural infrastructure and assets with the potential to contribute to sustainable livelihoods through wage employment. Thus, to understand the impact of the programme on the livelihood of the rural folk, the relationship between infrastructure development at the macro and micro level needs to be observed carefully and meticulously.

3

Research Model

A research model is designed with Infrastructure Development at Macro level (Asset A & D), Administrative Monitoring & Control, Social Justice, Environment Development and Public Health Care Systems as the independent variables that impact the Development of Rural Livelihood (Dependent Variable) of the rural folk participating in MGNREGS based on the research gap analysis in the Chapter 2.

3.1. Description of Dependent Variable

Development of Rural Livelihood could be measured by three items which are;

a. **Income Level** is an important determinant of one's economic prosperity and has a bearing on one's livelihood.
b. **Asset (B & D)** which could be measured by land productivity, horticulture, sericulture, fisheries and agricultural production.
c. **Social Status** could be measured by family education, social awareness and community relationship.

3.2. Description of Independent Variables

The study aims to measure the impact of the below-mentioned independent variables over the dependent variable that is development of Rural Livelihood.

a. **Infrastructure (Asset A & D)** could be quantifiably measured by the volume of work done in areas like water conservation, watershed management, afforestation and plantation, rural sanitation and Road connectivity.

b. **Good Governance** could measure by the intensity of Administrative Monitoring & Control in the surveyed areas.

c. **Social Justice** could be measured by the inertia of the Ombudsman, active grievance redressal and issues of the shed, wages administration and migration challenges.

d. **Environment Development** will be measured by the increase of green cover in the vicinity and drop in pollution level.

e. **The Public Health Care System** will be measured by the quality of services provided by the healthcare professionals, hygiene of the family and environment.

Fig No. 1 : Proposed Research Model

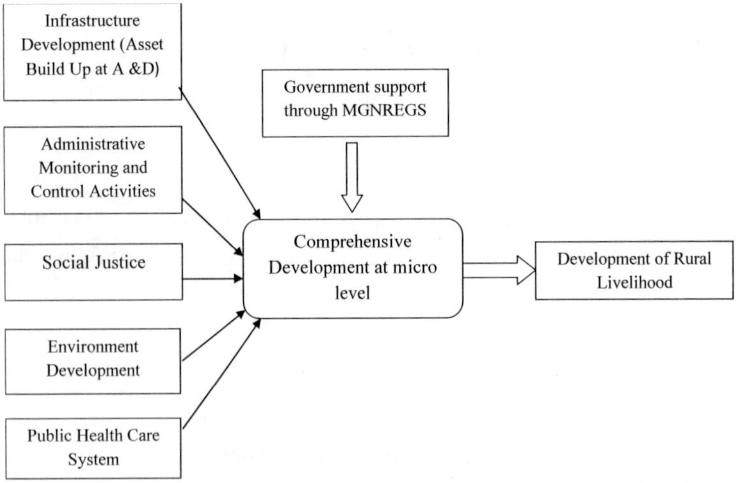

Further, the items to measure the dependent variable have been identified from the gap analysis which is placed below under Figure No. 2. The impact of the development of rural livelihood of marginal rural folk through their participation in MGNREGA could be seen in an increase in financial status; social status and asset build-up as these are the direct indicators of development. Hence, the second research model is proposed below :

Fig No. 2: Proposed Research Model

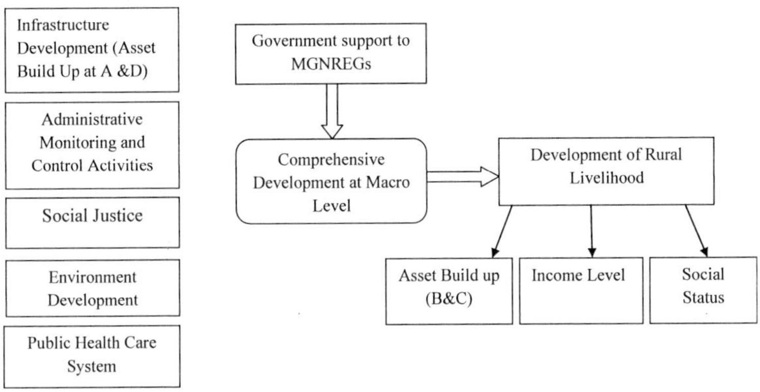

Therefore the proposed regression equation is

Variable Type	**Variable name**
Dependent Variable (DV):	Livelihood_Development
Independent Variable (IV):	Dev_Asset AD (IV_1), Admn_Ctrl (IV_2), Social_Just (IV_3), Env_Dev (IV_4), Pub_HealthCare (IV_5)

$$\mathbf{DV \leftarrow IV_1 + IV_2 + IV_3 + IV_4 + IV_5}$$

3.3. Hypotheses Development

Based on the research model described above, five hypotheses have been developed where the impact of independent variables of the model will be measured on the dependent variable. Since the study's objective is to measure the micro-level development at the village level under government support, these variables have been identified to realize the objectives.

H1: There is a significant positive association between the development of Rural Livelihood and Asset Build Up at the Macro level.

H2: Development of Rural Livelihood has a positive association with Administrative Monitoring & Control.

H3: Development of Rural Livelihood is significantly and positively associated with social justice.

H4: Development of Rural Livelihood and Environmental Development are significantly associated.

H5. There is a significant positive relationship between the development of Rural Livelihood and the public health care system.

3.4. Development Implication of the Relationship between Infrastructure Development and Rural Livelihood

The study has four encompassing limbs to focus on:

- Firstly, such a relationship has not been analysed in this region, and there is no literature, particularly on this topic.
- Secondly, MGNREGS is an essential component of the social and economic development of the country where implementing process/good governance has been playing a crucial role. Administrative monitoring and control of activities under MGNREGS by competent authorities be brought together in the form of an integrated package to better the social and economic situation of the people.
- Thirdly, the analysis is within the growing field of interest in government policy and its impact on the distribution of infrastructure. Several themes like infrastructural and institutional impact on social status, models of service provisions, and imbalanced development regarding infrastructure are embedded. The relationship between infrastructure development at the macro and micro levels was extracted, and its impact on rural livelihood was also be measured. The result of the analysis may be applied to maintain the balanced execution of MGNREGS for the development of rural livelihood at the macro and micro levels. The models could be made operational throughout the North-Eastern states at least on an experimental basis.

- Fourthly, the analysis will help to foresee the academicians associated with research work, as the present study group is a pioneer in this field because it takes intricate interviews, undertakes appropriate analysis, and uses statistical methods for assessing infrastructure and services on rural livelihood.

4

Research Methodology

4.1. Sampling Plan

All the eight districts of the state Tripura are considered for the analysis where disparity can be traced based on the allocation of infrastructure and services under MGNREGS and subsequently, two Panchayats of each block of each district was selected having the highest and lowest composite Z-score for micro-level study (Gaur and Archana, 1985). The composite Z-score provides the basis for assigning ranks to each Panchayat. The units having the highest composite Z-score were given 1st rank (Most Developed Panchayat) and the lowest (Least Developed Panchayat) composite Z-score was given the last rank.

To extract the good and concise research findings, 100 samples (maximum) each from MDP & LDP of all blocks of all districts were considered well-enough, and comparison which was done through a structured questionnaire for micro-level data analysis (Dillman, 2000 and Hill et. al. 2003). Random sampling technique is used for the study with a vigil for such areas where the above criteria were fulfilled.

4.2. Sampling Procedure:

Villages/Panchayats (Selected based on Z-score method)	Districts								Total Samples
	District-1	District-2	District-3	District-4	District-5	District-6	District-7	District-8	
MDP	100	100	100	100	100	100	100	100	800
LDP	100	100	100	100	100	100	100	100	800
Samples (Micro Level)	200	200	200	200	200	200	200	200	1600
Macro-Level data to be collected from all GPs & ADCs*									1039

Table 3 # Sample Distribution

State Statistics of Tripura (2014-2015)*
Districts: 8 Blocks: 58 Gram Panchayat & ADCs: 1039

Source: Ministry of Rural Development, GoI, 2015

4.3. Data Collection Instruments and Procedures

For identification of sample blocks and villages at the macro level, however, a Z-score test was applied on government data related to MGNREGS collected from various government offices through elected members/functionaries. Further, to provide a recommendation at State and Central levels. A random sampling method was administered for the study with a vigil for such areas where the above criteria should be fulfilled. The study was conducted to find out the impact of the MGNREGS on the Most Developed Panchayat (MDP) and Less Developed Panchayat (LDP) by collecting primary data with the help of a pre-framed questionnaire and adopting Focus Group Discussion, Semi-Structured Interview (SSI), and In-depth Interview.

4.4. Methodology for Analysis

The following analytical procedures were adopted to understand the relationship:

- The frequency of infrastructure occurrence under MGNREGS and their vicinity was counted using the Z-score method. The Z-score method depicts multi-dimensional growth, and structural changes in social systems, a new strategy of focusing attention upon certain favored places to achieve wider regional goals is now being increasingly advocated in many countries. Multiple regression analysis was used to specify the causes acting behind this dispersion. A series of in-depth focus group discussions were conducted to reveal the underlying facets hindering development with the stakeholders at different blocks.
- To satisfy the second objective, the multiple regression method was adopted. In multiple regression, the influence of multiple independent variables (here, we have five on the left-hand side of the model) on one dependent variable (here we have one manifested by three different items) was measured. To determine the impact of infrastructure development at the micro and macro level through MGNREGS participation on the Development of Rural Livelihood, the use of this statistical tool would provide a regression equation that could be applied in other states under similar situations. Further, government support works as a moderating variable; therefore, introducing a regression equation using a dummy variable is more suitable to attain the analysis outcome.
- Further, to formulate a comprehensive developmental plan, the Government and Rural Development Practitioners can take necessary steps based on Z-score, and provide required facilities to the Blocks/Panchayats/Villages.
- The Z-score method used for depicting the multi-dimensional growth and structural changes in social

systems has been adopted to identify the favored places and vice versa. To determine the rank of the settlements in terms of the cumulative value of the selected variables, the method of "Z-score" transformation has been used, which comprises the following formula :

$$\bar{x} = \Sigma x / N$$

$$(x - \bar{x})$$

$$\Sigma(x - \bar{x})^2$$

$$Standard\ Deviation\ (SD) = \sqrt{\Sigma(x - x)^2 / N}\ Zs =$$

$$Zs = (x - \bar{x}) / SD$$

$$Composite\ Zs = \Sigma Zs$$

$$R = Composite\ Zs$$

Where,

$$\bar{x} = \Sigma x / N = Mean = Total\ number\ of\ variables / Total\ number\ of\ units$$

$(x - \bar{x})$ = *Value of the variable – Mean of the Variable*

$\Sigma(x - \bar{x})^2$ = *Summation of* $(x - \bar{x})^2$

$\sqrt{\Sigma(x - \bar{x})^2/N}$ = *Standard Deviation of all variables*

$Zs = (x - \bar{x}) / SD$ *-score = Value of variable –Mean of the variable/Standard Deviation*

CZs = Zs = Computation of composite Z-score based on the total of Z-scores of 88 variables

R = CZs = Ranking of each panchayat based on the composite Z-score

1) The value of each variable in all the 1039 villages has been calculated and the mean value of each 88 variables has been computed separately.
2) $(X - \bar{X})$ of all the variables of all the villages have been computedby subtracting the mean of each variable from the original value of the variable in each unit.
3) $(X - \bar{X})^2$ of each variable for all units are totaled.
4) The Standard Deviation (S.D) of each variable has been computed.
5) The Z-score has been computed by dividing the $(X - \bar{X})$ of each variable of each unit by Standard Deviation.
6) The composite Z-Score has been computed by totaling the Z-score of 88 variables for each village.
7) The composite Z-score has been computed by totaling the Z-scores of 88 variables of each settlement. Finally, the Z-score provides the basis for assigning ranks to each of the villages. The units with the highest composite z-score are given the 1st rank, and the units with the lowest score are given the least rank (Gaur, Archana, 1985).
8) Multiple regression analysis was used to specify the causes acting behind this dispersion.

5

Descriptive Result and Discussion

5.1 Focus Group Discussions

The questionnaire was vetted through a Focused Group Discussion with a representative sample of 40 Gram Rozgar Sevak (GRS) (@ 5 GRS from each district). The details of the GRS are enlisted as Table 6 at Annexure-1. The district wise detailed outcomes of the FDG may be seen as under:

From the inception of MGNREGA in 2005 at India, a paradigm shift from earlier theories and programmes came into existence. With a legal framework and right-based approach, MGNREGS aims to enhance livelihood security by providing at least 100 days of guaranteed wage employment to the unskilled masses. A striving effort was initiated to generate a fruitful employment source for the weaker and marginalized sections of society and the development of rural assets. Despite every successful attempt made to reach out to the working sections, a detailed study was necessary to acquire a complete knowledge about the livelihood status of rural masses after the core implementation of the act in Tripura. Thus, a relative effort is made to sincerely analyze the core attributes of the livelihood development of rural masses in Tripura. Further, a prolonged effort is made to magnify the knowledge scale about the present scenario of the livelihood segment of the entire Tripura.

A planned approach was initiated to generate the parameters of study related to the Livelihood Assets, Good Governance, Social

Justice, Environmental Development & Rural Health Care System with a particular method of data collection, namely, Focused Group Discussion. Focused Group Discussion is frequently used as a qualitative approach to understand social issues in-depth. Thus, the programme aimed to gain an extensive level of knowledge through accumulating like-minded respondents serving in the MGNREGS.

Following a brief introduction about the programme and its necessary assets below given are a set of parameters based on Assets, Governance, Social Justice, Environmental Development & Health Care System which were discussed with the GRS (Gramin Rozgar Sevak).

1) Rural Livelihood Development Assets [B & C]

a) Increase in Land Productivity,

b) Increase in Horticulture,

c) Increase in Sericulture,

d) Increase in Fisheries,

e) Increase in Agriculture,

f) Increase in Income,

g) Increase in Social Status.

2) Infrastructure Development Assets [A & D]

a) Development of Roads,
b) Availability of Drinking water,
c) Availability of Household Materials,
d) Sanitation Facilities,
e) Improvement of Sanitation Facilities,
f) Improvement of Irrigation System,
g) Improvement of Water Conservation,
h) Improvement of Watershed Management,
i) Afforestation & Plantation.

3) Good Governance

a) Enhancement of Participation,
b) Enforcement of Rule of Law,
c) Maintaining Transparency,
d) Improvement in Efficiency,
e) Collective Decision Making,
f) Maintaining Equity,

g) Measuring Effectiveness and Efficiency,

h) Reduction of Debt,

i) Improvement in Consumption Level.

4) Social Justice

a) Informing the incidents to Ombudsman,

b) An active grievance cell,

c) False Redressal Issues,

d) Inertia of Wage Administration,

e) Gender Relations,

f) Rural Urban Migration,

g) Caste Segregation of Work,

h) Increased Social Skills of Women,

i) Enhancement and availability of Representatives.

5) Environmental Development

a) Increasing number of Trees,

b) Increasing number of Ponds,

c) Increasing Water levels of Ponds,

d) Increasing number of VATs/PITs.

6) Rural Health Care System

a) Rural Health Services,

b) Increase in number of Private Doctors,

c) Increase in the number of Doctors and Health Staffs in Government Hospital,

d) Increase in Hygiene of the Family,

e) Increase in Hygiene of the Environment,

f) Minimal Availability of Medicine in Local Hospital,

g) Clinical Test facility available in PHC/private Hospital,

h) Health Condition of the family.

The respondents, namely the GRS (Gramin Rozgar Sevak) were selected randomly based on 8 districts of Tripura.

5.2. Outcomes of the Focused Group Discussion (FGD)

The discussions were conducted depending on the above-given parameters focusing on the activities carried out by the GRS. Each one of them representing the eight districts shared their consent about the parameters, which are segmented below:

5.2.1. Gomati District

a) **Assets (B&C):** According to the respondent, the agricultural farming in Gomati District presently focuses on agriculture at low lands of the district rather than in the hills or hillocks. They suggested that the concept of **Terrace Farming** should be implemented in the hilly regions along with a growing variety of crops in it for better output over the whole year. They also added that the plants grown over the hilly sections can be taken care of by the elderly persons and the community's youths registered within MGNREGA.

b) **Assets (A&D):** They said that for the betterment of the environmental ecosystem, more plants should be grown in all the parts of the region, especially plants like Amla, Haritaki (Bohera), etc.

c) **Good Governance:** For better governance, they suggested some points which are enlisted below:

   i. After successful filling of the **Fund Transfer Order (FTO)**, the requisite amount of money should be paid by the government **within 15 days** of their activity,

   ii. The **Bank Correspondent** (**BC**) model of payment should be implemented without further delay to stop the irregularities in distributing the funds.

d) **Social Justice:** On the part of Social Justice, Mr. Bose added the following points:

   i. Every year, a workshop on Financial Analysis on the implementation of the MGNREGA work in Gram Panchayats should be organized along with analysing the outcomes of such implementation,

ii. In the case of Social Audit, M.S. Book should be provided from each block.

e) **Environmental Development:** Excavation of ponds can be done within two years of its formation.

f) **Rural Health Care:** Under the Scheme of Swachh Bharat Abhiyan, biodegradable and non-biodegradable wastes can be collected from dustbins and used as fertilizers.

5.2.2. West Tripura District

a) **Assets (B&C):** Construction of shelters for the cattle and birds focusing on the **Bower System.**

b) **Assets (A&D):** The salient points were described by the group of GRS, which are described below:

i. Iron Free Drinking water,

ii. Preparation of River Dam,

iii. Construction of Rajiv Gandhi Sewa Kendra,

iv. Anganwadi Centre,

v. Construction of Switch Gate,

vi. Construction of Box Culvert,

vii. Construction of Pucca Drain.

c) **Good Governance:** The points are highlighted below:

i. Delay of Payment,

ii. Improper information among the residents on availability of Funds in GP,

iii. Specification of wages delivery system in workers single bank account under the supervision of Gram Panchayat,

iv. Poor Connectivity of Internet and Shortage of Computer,

v. Frequency of Social Audit to be increased, i.e. within every 6 months or 1year,

vi. A distinct report on Population to be acquired,

vii. A Periodic Work List entitled with all the previous works,

viii. Job Card wise Family ID.

d) **Environment Development:** The points are given below:

i. Recharge Pit,

ii. Water Recharge Pit,

iii. Roadside plantation.

e) **Rural Health Care:** The points are given below:

i. Ambulance facilities in all the PHC,

ii. 24 hours doctor facilities in PHC.

5.2.3. Dhalai District

a) Assets (B&C): According to the respondents, various other departments have been merged with MGNREGA namely;

i. **Tripura Tea Development Corporation (TTDC):** The TTDC has been merged with the MGNREGS to reach the rural areas of Tripura, especially the tea farming areas.

ii. **Tripura Tribal Area Autonomous District Council (TTAADC):** The TTAADC also incorporated necessary steps to merge its activities with the MGNREGS to develop the livelihood structure of the residents of ADC (Autonomous District Council) villages as Rubber Plantation, Areca Nut farming, Banana, Cassava etc.

iii. Tripura Rubber Plantation Corporation (TRPC): The Rubber Plantation in various districts are linked with the MGNREGA, i.e., collection of latex through proper division and formation of its by-products.

iv. **Primitive Tribal Groups (PTG):** The Primitive Tribal Groups are also merged with MGNREGA to function in the aspects of plantation and similar other activities.

b) **Assets (A&D):** The points are given below:

   i. The layering of bricks/AAC blocks in the roads,

   ii. Construction of Pucca Culvert,

   iii. Construction of AWC,

   iv. Construction of RGSK (Rajiv Gandhi Sewa Kendra).

c) **Good Governance:** The points are given below:

   i. Financial Incapability to produce jobs,

   ii. Regularization of Social Audit.

d) **Environmental Development:**

   i. Implementation of Individual Household Latrine Application (IHHL).

e) **Rural Health Care Service**

   i) Shortage of Doctors,

   ii) Non-Availability of Medicine.

Recommendations

- Bio-metric Attendance System,
- Roadside Tree Plantation,
- Construction of C.C. Block road,
- Pure Water Distribution,
- Proper water facility for IHHL,
- Maintenance up to 3 years for MGNREGA in tree plantation.

5.2.4. South Tripura District

a) **Assets (B&C):** The salient points shared are highlighted below:

i. Convergence of Agriculture & MGNREGS,

ii. Convergence of ARDD & MGNREGS,

iii. Convergence of TRLM & MGNREGS,

iv. Forest up-gradation.

b) Assets (A&D): The salient points are given below:

i. Convergence of MGNREGS and PWD,

ii. Improvement of Kaccha Road,

iii. Agri-Land Development,

iv. Kitchen Garden.

c) Good Governance: The salient points are given below:

i. Ease in Payment system,

ii. Proper labour budget,

iii. Engagement of requisite staff at all the MGNREGA department,

iv. Smooth Cooperation among all the departments.

d) **Social Justice:** The salient points are given below:

   i. Inspection of Record Register on Social Audit within every six months,

   ii. Provision of better health facilities for the workers,

   iii. Child Care Centre or Creche Centre to be introduced,

   iv. Proper shed facility near the worksites.

e) **Environmental Development:** The salient points are given below:

   i. Formation of Compost Pit,

   ii. Initiation of Dustbins in Household Level,

   iii. Proper functioning of IHHL.

f) **Rural Health Care:** The salient points are given below:

   i. One specialized doctor in every PHC,

   ii. Enrolment of Job card holders within PMJAY (Pradhan Mantri Jan Arogya Yojana).

Recommendations:

- Provision of Financial Support to 30 MGNREGA workers every year on focusing at the interest level of the workers.

5.2.5. Sepahijala District

a) **Assets (B&C):** The salient points given below are provided by the respondents:

   i. **Animal Resource Development Department (ARDD)** has been integrated into the MGNREGS in which extensive veterinary health coverage is provided to the livestock's and birds along with plantation of grasses and similar other products for the growth and development of the livestock.

   ii. **Aquaculture Farming Tanks** in household level.

   iii. Provision of lending money from farming until harvesting.

   iv. **Bamboo** Seed Distribution at the household level.

b) **Assets (A&D):** The salient points are given below:

   i. Land Leveling at an Individual Level and through Community Organization,

   ii. Metalling & Carpeting of Roads,

   iii. Provision of Roadside Pucca Drains.

c) **Good Governance:** The salient points are given below:

   i. Observation by State level Monitoring Committee,

   ii. Online Job card entry and linking of bank passbook,

   iii. Bio-metric attendance.

d) **Social Justice:** The salient points are given below:

   i. **Social Audit**: Household visit along with other audit facilities to be increased in parallel to the increase of responsibilities of Gram Pradhan.

e) **Environmental Development:** The salient points are given below:

   i. Research Pit to be initiated within the rubber plantation areas,

   ii. River side tree plantation,

   iii. Anti-Soil Projection of Soil Erosion.

f) **Rural Health Care:** The salient points are given below:

   i. Participation of ASHA workers,

   ii. Health Insurance for Job card holders and GRS,

   iii. Inclusion of PMJAY with MGNREGA,

   iv. The death penalty of any workers or GRS should be dealt with by the Govt. body.

Recommendations:

- Minimum 100 days work must be mandatory,
- Job guarantee of GRS,
- Increase of Time Limit for the workers,
- Maternity facility to be provided to MGNREGA female workers.

5.2.6. Unakoti District

a) **Assets (B&C):** The salient points given below are provided by the respondents:

   i. Terrace Farming,

   ii. Compost Pit,

   iii. ARDD scheme.

b) **Assets (A&D):** The salient points are given below:

   i. AWC kitchen shed

c) **Good Governance:** The salient points are given below:

i. Ease of Wage Disbursement among workers,

ii. Daily payment provisions,

iii. Provision of basic logistics,

iv. An independent department for MGNREGA must be formed.

d) **Environmental Development:** The salient points are given below:

   i. IHHL (Individual Household Latrine Application),

   ii. **Social Audit:** Register Maintenance, Worker's Output, PMJAY scheme implementation, Social Pension, Social Discussion,

   iii. **Solar Panel Inclusion** in all the villages to save the Environment.

5.2.7. Khowai District

a) **Assets (B&C):** The salient points given below are provided by the respondents:

   i. ARDD (Animal Resource Development Department),

   ii. TTAADC sub zonal Tea Plantation.

b) **Assets (A&D):** The salient points are given below:

   i. Flood protection,

   ii. Trance Cutting of Jhum Cultivated Plants.

c) **Good Governance:** The salient points are given below:

   i. Availability of FTO,

   ii. Aadhar Activation on Job cards,

   iii. Resolution of Gram Sabha Resolution Register,

   iv. Formation of Action Plan wise Activities,

   v. Work site visit and provision of Technical Inputs in the area,

   vi. Management of File on Cash dispersal among the workers.

d) **Rural Health Care:**

i. Provision of Health Care facility,

ii. Provision of Medical Laboratory,

iii. Awareness camps on various type of diseases.

Recommendations

- Road side ethno-medicine plantation,
- Maintenance of irrigation,
- Maintenance of water harvesting,
- Administrative charge to be provided to Gram Panchayats,
- Development of village level road with brick and C.C. block carpeting.

5.2.8. North Tripura District

a) Assets (B&C): The salient points given below are provided by the respondents:

i. Agricultural land to be brought under MGNREGA,

ii. ARDD with proper maintenance of animal,

iii. Recharge Pit inclusion at the household level.

b) Assets (A&D): The salient points are given below:

i. Road side Jungle cutting,

ii. Formation of roadside drain.

c) Environmental Development: The salient points are given below:

i. Compost Pit at household level,

ii. Community dustbin.

d) Social Justice: The salient points are given below:

i. Job security of personnel linked directly with MGNREGS

e) **Good Governance:** The salient features are given below:

   i. Internet Facility along with Wi-Fi is the utmost priority for this Block,

   ii. No computer facility available.

5.3. Livelihood Development of West Tripura

5.3.1 Introduction

Training can be described explicitly as a process of developing oneself through enhancing one's capacity, capability, productivity and performance. It simply shows a way for the overall development of an individual. With a complete focus on the livelihood conditions of the rural residents, a concrete study is made to receive briefings about the current situation of MGNREGS applicability in West Tripura.

West Tripura is the administrative capital of Tripura, it gets more emphasized as the only Municipal Corporation and Capital city of Tripura lies in this district. West Tripura District comprises three sub-divisions: Sadar Subdivision, Mohanpur Subdivision and Jirania Subdivision. Moreover, the district has 9 blocks, namely, Bamutia, Belbari, Dukli, Hezamara, Jirania, Lefunga, Mandai, Mohanpur and Old Agartala, covering a total number of 87 Gram Panchayats and 85 ADC villages. MGNREGS was implemented in West Tripura district from 2008, which sequentially became a great boon for the unskilled classes, as searching for daily labour opportunities declined with time. MGNREGS not only generated a good source of income but also tried to give a boost to livelihood development. The programme was initiated to assess the Gram Panchayats lying under different blocks of West Tripura District. The data collection method was through questionnaire, as a meso-level understanding of the facts and figures can be fetched about the implementation of the MGNREGS in the whole district. Thus, the Pradhan/President of all the Gram Panchayats were invited. A discussion was carried out on the implementation of MGNREGS in their vicinity. They were provided with a set of questionnaires. Thus, an extensive effort is made to analyze the effects of MGNREGS through a quantitative study regarding the development of the livelihood status of the rural masses in the West Tripura District.

5.3.2 Activities carried out

With a sincere attempt on the topic, a systematic programme was organized to understand the present implementation scenario of MGNREGS in parts of West Tripura District. The Gram Panchayat Pradhans were the respondents and the list of which may be seen in Table-7 at Annexure-2.

With a proper understanding of the application of the MGNREGS in the West District, the team made a format to analyze the facts and figures of all the Gram Panchayats through the questionnaire, a basic level of data has been acquired which will be analyzed and concluding points were generated on these points. The programme ended successfully after proper collection of all the above-mentioned points.

5.3.3. Summary of the Program

The training programme for the Pradhan of the Gram Panchayats was initiated with a complete focus on assessing the livelihood conditions of the rural masses. The program was organised on the 21st December 2019 at Panchayati Raj Training Institute, West Tripura District.

From the beginning of the programme, a planned procedure was formulated to acquire all types of data related to the variables of the questionnaire. The program was initiated from 10:30 am till 4:30 pm. The questionnaire was explained by one of the team members to the Pradhans. They duly filled up a total number of 88 variables along with some other additional questions that were also raised for clarification of queries by them. Some of the Pradhans had a distinct understanding of their Gram Panchayats, whereas others were new to the post and took time to appreciate the matters. A total of 62 Panchayat Pradhans were present in the programme.

The entire program was carried out decently with a twin motive to get a complete idea about the Panchayats and develop a strong rapport with the Pradhans of those Panchayats. Various other social issues and matters came out about the Panchayats. A conclusion can be drawn that the acting governing bodies will be much affirmative in gaining the targets that are ensured for the betterment of the society.

5.4. Livelihood Development of Gomati District

5.4.1. Introduction

Orientation means the initiation of someone to the present adaptability condition of the surroundings. The programme was organized to get a brief understanding of the prevailing developmental conditions of the Gomati District. A sincere attempt is made to analyze the facts and figures of the resources present in the Gram Panchayats of Gomati District.

Gomati District is one of the new districts among eight other Tripura districts formed in 2012. The name 'Gomati' evolved from the river Gomati, the biggest river in Tripura. The District Headquarter of Gomati District is Udaipur, which is an indigenous place for the residents of Tripura. This district is also covered with famous ethnic and traditional spots made by the emperors of Tripura, namely, Tripura Sundari Temple and Amar Sagar. Moreover, various other eco-parks, lakes, and libraries also attract tourists from different parts of the country. Gomati District comprises 3 subdivisions: Udaipur, Amarpur and Karbook, which are sub-divided into 8 blocks covering 75 Gram Panchayats and 98 ADC villages. The data collection method was through a questionnaire, which gave some basic ideas about the resources present at each of their villages in the vicinity of the Panchayat Pradhan. Thus, a strategic step is forwarded towards gaining some knowledge about the developmental status of the villages under the Gomati Districts. The MGNREGS got its applicability in the Gomati District before the formation of the new district, i.e., the Act earlier got the platform of South Tripura District. So, an effort is made to understand the overall resource generation and maintenance of those with a focus on the all-around development of the Panchayats.

5.4.2. Activities Carried Out

The effort to analyze the present situation of the implementation of MGNREGS in the Gomati District has been actualized by collecting the resource-based data through the questionnaire. The Pradhans of Gram Panchayats under the Gomati District successfully contributed to meso-level data collection through questionnaire. The program ended successfully with proper quantitative data collection, and the process would result in the formation of an excellent report on the impact of MGNREGS in the livelihood development of Tripura.

5.4.3. Summary of the Program

The orientation programme was organized on the premises of Panchayati Raj Training Institute, Gomati District. Out of 75 Gram Panchayats, 60 Panchayat Pradhans were present in the programme and the list may be seen as Table-8 at Annexure-2.

The program's initiation was carried on while keeping in mind the roots of the discussion, especially acquiring the panchayat level data and building a good rapport with the Pradhans. The prime intent of the program was fulfilled when a requisite response through the questionnaire was successfully gathered. Several patterns of questions followed by their queries were highlighted by the respondents, which were described profoundly by the researchers. The programme became a successful one resulting in developing a comfortable condition for the respondents to fill up the questionnaire.

Various issues regarding the situations of Gram Panchayats came out and some demands have been put in the questionnaire regarding the development of the villages. Thus, the programme was ended with successful data collection regarding the livelihood conditions of the rural masses of the Gomati District.

5.5. Livelihood Development of South Tripura District

5.5.1. Introduction

Data collection can be described as a process by which information gathered can be measured on targeted variables in a system, which then helps evaluate the outcomes of the study. A preliminary approach has been initiated towards enabling the process of data collection through a questionnaire. To identify the developmental strategies taken by the Panchayats through the implementation of MGNREGS in the areas of South Tripura District, a brief activity was the need of an hour. Thus, a sequential step was kept forward to acknowledge some structure of the village development patterns.

South Tripura District came into existence in the year 1970, when the whole state of Tripura was divided into 3 districts. Presently, the state has eight districts and the South Tripura District covers a total area of 1514.3 sq.km. The present district headquarters of South Tripura is Belonia. The District consists of 3 sub-divisions: Santirbazar, Belonia and Sabroom. Moreover, the district has 8 Rural Development Blocks and 3 Nagar Panchayats, under which there are 90 Gram Panchayats and 70 ADC villages. The implementation of MGNREGS in the South Tripura came into existence in 2008, when the Act got its full applicability over all the states of India. Thus, with an efficient effort to move out the exact scenario of the rural infrastructure, a sound and definite step has been developed to get a concrete idea about the livelihood conditions of the rural masses, especially the workers and beneficiaries.

5.5.2. Activities Carried Out

The livelihood conditions of the rural masses have been assessed based on the recording of the questionnaire capturing the inputs provided by the Gram Panchayat Pradhan enlisted as Table-8 at Annexure-3. The information provided was reasonable to get a clear idea about the Panchayats lying in their respected vicinity.

5.5.3. Summary of the Program

The program was organized in Panchayati Raj Training Institute, Gomati District in Udaipur on 24th December. The Panchayat *Pradhan* of various Blocks of South Tripura District were invited for this program. 66 Pradhans were present. It began with an introduction about the role of MGNREGS in developing rural attire. The Panchayat Pradhans present in the program responded about the prevailing situation on MGNREGS in their areas.

Several questions were raised relating to Health, Sanitation and Transportation during the filling up of questionnaires. The questions represented well existence of the programme and the demand for work in the Panchayat areas. However, the Panchayat Pradhans made an efficient effort to provide the exact number of resources present in the community. The programme was handled in a proper manner, and the respondents filled the lists of variables given through questionnaires. A continuous evaluation was done in the pretext of attaining a clear and sound report about the livelihood conditions prevalent in the Gram Panchayats.

'*Positivity needs no cause when one inhibits it within himself*', this was observed in all the Pradhans of the Gram Panchayat to mitigate all the prevailing problems existing in their respective Gram Panchayats. The researchers found a determined trend within the respondents to develop their Panchayats and make it a model for the rest of the State.

5.6. Livelihood Development of Sepahijala District

5.6.1. Introduction

'Sepahijala' is a newly born district with all kinds of attractive tourist spots, like Neer Mahal, Sepahijala Wildlife Sanctuary, Kamalasagar Kali Temple (preferably named Koshba Kalibari) is one of the most visited places in Tripura. The district has a total area covering 1043.4 sq. km. The District Headquarter is situated in Bishramganj. Within its vast area, the district has 3 sub-divisions namely, Bishalgarh, Sonamura and Jampuijala.

Moreover, the district has 7 blocks covering 111 Gram Panchayats and 58 ADC villages. The imposition of MGNREGA was under West Tripura District in the year 2008 before its formation as an independent district and 3 other districts. From the date of applicability of MGNREGA, it has successfully contributed to the overall development of the whole state. Various studies have been carried out based on several implementation strategies of MGNREGA. Still, this study of assessing the Livelihood Development of the beneficiaries is preferably an out-of-the-text attempt by the researchers. Through this study, a clear image of developmental attributes initiated through MGNREGA by the authorities of the Gram Panchayats will be visible. Thus, the researchers have selected a pattern to understand the meso level structure of development by forming questionnaires and gaining concrete knowledge about the Panchayats.

5.6.2. Activities Carried Out

To foster the idea of gaining a better knowledge about the implementation structure of the MGNREGS in the villages, a set of questionnaires were prepared along with some residual information have been sorted out. The above information thus collected is purely based on the details shared by the Panchayat Pradhan of different blocks of Sepahijala District. The list of Pradhanshas been appended in Table-9 at Annexure-4. The Panchayat Pradhan collaborated decently and provided the required information through the questionnaire.

5.6.3. Summary of the Program

On 31st January 2019, a workshop on the impact of MGNREGS in rural livelihood development of Tripura was organized on the premises of Panchayati Raj Training Institute, West Tripura District. The vital aim of the programme was to assess the livelihood conditions of the rural masses under various Gram Panchayats.

The programme was organized with a steep motivation to understand the application of MGNREGS and its outcomes that could be exploited to develop the rural masses. Out of 111 Gram Panchayats, 89 respondents were present with full zeal and enthusiasm in the program. The respondents sequentially filled the questionnaires while raising some questions regarding the availability of the resources in their community. The activity carried on through the program resulted in getting a concrete idea about the conditions of the villages. The programme ended successfully with the collection of accurate data and information.

5.7. Livelihood Development of North Tripura District

5.7.1. Introduction

North Tripura District is one of the oldest districts in Tripura. The only route that connects Tripura with all the other states of India passes within the North Tripura. Since 1987, North Tripura District got its identity as the sole administrative part of the major hilly regions of Tripura. With time, the district was bifurcated into two viz; Dhalai (1995) and Unakoti (2012). Earlier, the administrative headquarter of District was situated in Kailashahar. But, after its further division in the year 2012, the present headquarter got shifted to Dharmanagar.

North Tripura District covers several hilly regions that are homes for various indigenous people. The total area of North Tripura District is 1422.19 sq. km, with a total population of 4, 44,579. The North Tripura District is sub-divided into three sub-divisions, namely, Dharmanagar, Panisagar and Kanchanpur. These three sub-divisions cover eight RD Blocks, specifically Kalacherra, Laljuri, Jubarajnagar, Kadamtala, Dasda, Jampui Hills, Panisagar, Damcherra. The total number of Gram Panchayat and Village Committees governed by the Blocks are 129. The implementation of MGNREGS started from its inception, i.e., from the year 2008. With their complete focus on identifying the development margin of MGNREGS implementation, the team of researchers went to the respective areas to collect the data from the village administration. Moreover, the Block Administration also induced its helping hand to gather the requisite information from the aforementioned Panchayats and Village Committees.

5.7.2. Activities Carried Out

The livelihood conditions of the rural masses were assessed based on the recording of responses to the questionnaire administered on the *Pradhans* of the Gram Panchayats. The list of Pradhans may be seen in Table-10 at Annexure-5. The Unakoti District Administration provided the secondary data. The information generated gave a clear idea about the GP/VC lying under their jurisdiction.

5.7.3. Summary of the Programme

The data collection was carried out within a stipulated time, and all the requisite information were collected from different blocks, which are explained below:

a) **Damcherra:** Damcherra is situated in one of the hilly regions of North Tripura. It is situated 59 km (approx.) from its District Headquarter Dharmanagar. Damcherra, ultimately comes under Autonomous District Council (ADC) area. The Block administration comes under Mr. Pijush Deb, BDO, Damcherra RD Block. Under his guidance, the research team met with all the Village Committee Chairpersons and gathered the necessary information according to the questionnaire format. Moreover, Mr. Deb also shared some insights which would render in the development of the whole area under the implementation guidelines of MGNREGA. The total number of Village Committees across the entire area is 13.

b) **Dasda:** Dasda Block lies almost in the outermost part of the North Tripura District. Its complete distance from the district headquarter is 65 km (approx). Dasda has an equal number of tribal population along with the local Bengali population. This place remains completely sensitive as it earlier had refugee camps within it. The local administration comes under the aegis of Mr. Saikat Saha, BDO, Dasda RD Block. Under his advice, the team met with the Panchayat Pradhan & Village Committee Chairperson's to gather requisite information about the implementation range of MGNREGA in their area. The entire Block has 11 Gram Panchayat and 6 Village Committees.

c) **Jampui Hills:** Jampui Hills can be considered the gateway to heaven in North Tripura District. It lies almost lies 90 km from its district headquarter, Dharmanagar. The hills section does have attractive spots that gather tourists from every end of the state to visit it. The Block is also famous for its oranges which are much tasty compared to other areas. Mr. Kishore Sarkar, BDO, Jampui Hills, is at the helm of the management of the administrative activities of the block. Through his guidance, the team met with all the village committee chairpersons and gathered all the information from them as per the questionnaire that was set previously. The total number of village committees in Jampui Block are seven.

d) **Jubarajnagar:** Jubarajnagar Block is the nearest block that lies within the district headquarter, Dharmanagar. The block lies in the low land area which has agriculture as the utmost priority of the local citizens. The Block Administration is run by Mr. Anupam Das, BDO, Jubarajnagar RD Block. Under his able suggestion, the team made a sincere attempt to gather all the detailed information from the Panchayats and Village committees. The total number of Panchayats and Village Committees are 23.

e) **Kadamtala:** Kadamtala lies near the Assam-Tripura Border which is the only route that connects Tripura with Assam and all the other states of Tripura. Kadamtala Block is administered by Mr. Kamal Debbarma, BDO, Kadamtala RD Block. The research team attempted to understand the scenario of the implementation of MGNREGA in the area of Kadamtala Block. The total number of Panchayat is 19.

f) **Kalacherra:** Kalacherra Block administers all the Panchayat that lies within the vicinity of the district headquarter. The Kalacherra RD Block is a newly developed block that was formed in the year 2012. The administrative authority is Mr. Tarun Kanti Sarkar, BDO, Kalacherra RD Block. The researchers made sincere attempts to analyze and gather all the requisite information from the villages under the aegis of Mr. Sarkar. The total number of Panchayat is 17.

g) **Laljuri:** Laljuri is a new rural development block declared in 2012, after the division of the North Tripura District into Unakoti District. Laljuri Block is almost 45 km from the district headquarter. The road condition over the whole area remained terrible during the whole process of data collection. The local administration strictly lies in the hands of Mr. Pinku Debbarma, BDO, Laljuri RD Block. The researchers had to visit twice in the area for the collection of requisite data from the areas. The total number of Panchayat and Village Committees are 13.

h) **Panisagar:** Panisagar is a newly formed sub-division under North Tripura District. Though, the area also has a block under its governance for the villages. The administration of the whole block area comes under Mr. Homagni Bhattacharjee, BDO, Panisagar, RD Block. Under the sincere guidance of Mr. Bhattacharjee, the researchers took the opportunity to visit the Panchayat and Village committees to render all the detailed information from them regarding the present scenario of the MGNREGA implementation in the whole area. The total number of Panchayats and Village Committees are 18.

5.8. Livelihood Development of Unakoti District

5.8.1. Introduction

'Unakoti' is a Bengali term that means 'one less than a crore'. The name of the District 'Unakoti' got its significance from its holy insights where 99, 99,999 sculptured idols of various Gods and Goddesses exist. The Archaeological Survey of India has declared it as a historically religious tourist spot for every individual. Before the bifurcation of North Tripura District until 2012, Unakoti was considered as a part of the district.

5.8.2. Activities Carried Out

The term 'Data' signifies the collection of facts and statistics which are collected together for reference or analysis. Thus, the research team attempted to collect all the necessary information from the respective Gram Panchayat Pradhans of all the Blocks underlying within the Unakoti District. Unakoti District is an assemblage of two sub-divisions, namely, Kailashahar and Kumarghat covering four blocks: Chandipur, Gournagar, Pencharthal, and Kumarghat. These four blocks have a total number of 59 Gram Panchayats and 32 ADC villages. The implementation of MGNREGS in the present Unakoti District started before its inception as a new District, i.e., from 2008. Thus, it can be cited that through a deliberate and sincere attempt, the accurate reflection of the MGNREGS work that has been carried out to date has been gathered equivalently. The unique model of the new district eased the purpose of the research team to meet the necessary Block Administration and gather all the details in the presence of the Gram Panchayat administration.

With the help of the structured questionnaire, livelihood conditions of the rural masses were assessed based on the recording of the questionnaire The list of Pradhans as per Table-11 at Annexure-6 facilitated the collection process.

5.8.3. Summary of the Program

The programmes were organized sequentially from 2nd March to 6th March 2020. The details of the programme carried out in the respective blocks are hereby described below:

a) **Chandipur Block:** Under the administration of Mr. Pradip Debbarma, BDO, Chandipur RD Block, the research team met with all the Gram Panchayat Pradhan's and Village Committee Chairperson's to gather all the requisite information regarding the interest of the project. This Block covers a total number of 14 Gram Panchayats and 4 Village committees. The research team made sincere attempts to cover all the areas of the information necessary to complete the meso-level data.

b) **Gournagar Block:** With permission from Mr. Manoj Kumar Saha, BDO, Gournagar RD Block, the team made efficient efforts to accumulate the information based on the dispatched questionnaire through the hands of the village administration. This Block covers a total number of 20 Gram Panchayats and 3 Village Committees. Mr. Saha helped the team gather all the detailed information about the trends in the development of livelihood under the implication of MGNREGA.

c) **Pecharthal Block:** Pencharthal Block is entirely covered by the Autonomous District Council area, where majorly the indigenous tribes exist. The office of Block Administration is run by Mr. Shyamajoy Jamatia, BDO, Pencharthal RD Block. Under the aegis of his administration, the development of all the village committees completely depends on him. The research team made a sincere effort to collect all the information from 16 Village Committees that are present within the vicinity of the Block.

d) **Kumarghat Block:** Kumarghat Block is the largest block under Unakoti District, which has 25 Gram Panchayats and 9 Village Committees. The team has collected all the information from the Panchayats mentioned above and Committees. The Kumarghat Block is administered by Mr. Mithun Das Choudhury, BDO, Kumarghat Block.

The information collected above was the meso-level information required to identify the Most Developed Panchayat (MDP) and Least Developed Panchayat (LDP) amongst all the district panchayats to be identified for further micro-level analysis.

6

Analytical Results and Discussions

6.1. Z-Score Calculation

The study identified the following 8 Most Developed Panchayats (MDPs) and 8 Least Developed Panchayats *(LDPs)* based on the Z-Score from each of the Districts in the State.

6.2. Micro-Level Data Analysis

The study aims to reveal if there is any significant relationship between the Rural Livelihood Development in Tripura through MGNERS work and the contributing factors like Asset Build up at the macro level, Administrative Monitoring & Control, Social Justice, and Environmental Development & Public Healthcare System.

6.3. Regression Analysis

As per the review of extant literature, it has been found that the development of rural livelihood is influenced by five independent variables, which were measured by 47 items, and thus the following regression equation is posited,

Rural Livelihood Development = B0 + B1 Asset Build up at the macro level + B2 Administrative Monitoring & Control + B3 Social Justice + B4 Environmental Development +B5 Public Healthcare System.

Sl. No	DISTRICTS	GRAM PANCHAYAT				
		MDP	Composite Z-Score	LDP	Composite Z-Score	District Code for Micro-Level Data Analysis
1	North Tripura	**Kalagangerpar** Kadamtala Block	1.306	**Rowa,** Panisagar Block	0.058	2
2	Unokoti	**Bilashpur,** Chandipur Block	0.112	**Bagaicherra,** Pencharthal Block	-0.33	7
3	Gomati	**Mailak,** Amarpur Block	0.33	**Rangamati,** Amarpur Block	0.0001	5
4	South Tripura	**Chittamara,** B.C. Nagar Block	0.047	**Gouranga Bazar,**Rajnagar Block	-0.917	8
5	Khowai	**PurbaChebri,** Khowai Block	0.498	**Gournagar** Khowai Block	-2.49	3
6	Sepahijala	**Bordowal,** Nalchar Block	0.272	**Nabinnagar,** Bishalgarh Block	-3.509	6

Table-4: District wise MDPs and LDPs

	District1	District 2	District 3	District 4	District 5	District 6	District 7	District 8	Tripura State
Cronbach Alpha	0.788	0.748	0.749	0.779	0.810	0.812	0.799	0.776	0.788
Items#	6	6	6	6	6	6	6	6	6
N	200	200	200	200	200	200	200	202	1602

Table-5: Reliability Statistics

The instrument's reliability was conducted, and the value of Cronbach's Alpha was calculated at a different point for the different number of collected samples. The final value of Cronbach's Alpha is 0.788 for N= 1602, covering the entire sample size, which is good to run the next series of tests.

Before running the tests for regression, necessary tests for normality were conducted and by using the two-step data normalization method of fractional rank calculation followed by inverse data function, the data sets were normalized, which can be seen from the P-P plot.

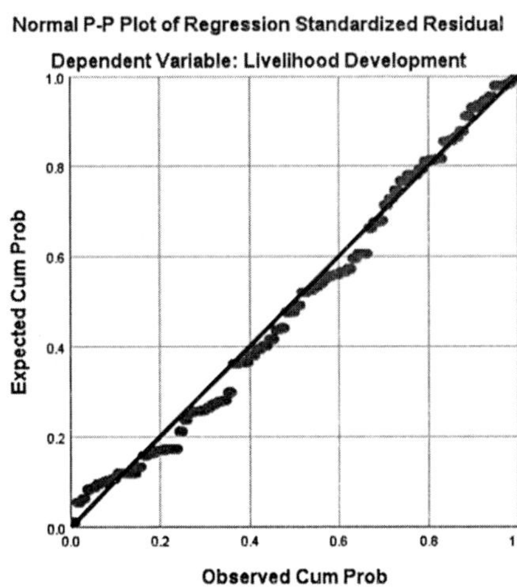

Fig. 3: P- P Plot

The Histogram below shows the normal distribution of data:

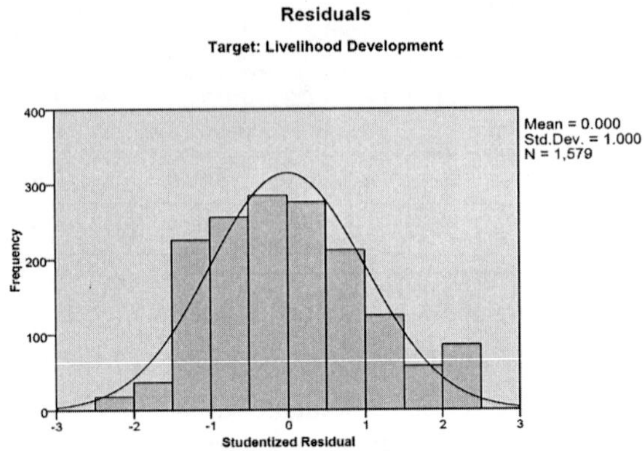

Fig. 4: Histogram showing Skewness & Kurtosis

	District 1	District 2	District 3	District 4	District 5	District 6	District 7	District 8	Tripura State
Adj R^2	0.565	0.601	0.594	0.536	0.622	0.611	0.534	0.627	0.597
Sig	0.000	0.000	0.000	0.000	0.000	0.000	0.000	0.000	0.000
Durbin-Watson	1.624	1.684	1.678	1.664	1.587	1.536	1.615	1.660	1.692
Items#	6	6	6	6	6	6	6	6	6
N	200	200	200	200	200	200	200	202	1602

a. Dependent Variable: Livelihood Development

b. Predictors: (Constant), Public Health Service, Environment Development, Admn Monitor Control, Asset Development, Social Justice

Table-6 : Significance of the Model

Since the model is significant ($p<0.05$), the respective regression equations and corresponding coefficients must be checked to develop the best fit regression equation. The regression co-efficient tables are presented below overall as well as district-wise for better clarity. Moreover, the Durbin-Watson value is between 1.5 to 2.5, making it a fit case to run the linear regression analysis.

District 1

Model		Standardized Coefficients	t	Sig.	
		Beta			VIF
1	(Constant)	-.358	-.947	.345	
	Asset Development	-.114	-1.708	.089	2.023
	Admn Monitor Control	.286	4.006	.000	2.338
	Social Justice	.546	7.597	.000	2.365
	Environment Development	.185	3.812	.000	1.076
	Public Health Service	-.056	-.971	.333	1.537

District 2

Model		Standardized Coefficients	t	Sig.	
		Beta			VIF
1	(Constant)	-.404	-1.071	.285	
	Asset Development	-.207	-3.734	.000	1.498
	Admn Monitor Control	.324	4.686	.000	2.331
	Social Justice	.539	7.802	.000	2.326
	Environment Development	.171	3.624	.000	1.085
	Public Health Service	-.015	-.305	.760	1.212

District 3

Model		Standardized Coefficients	t	Sig.	
		Beta			VIF
1	(Constant)	-.403	-1.067	.287	
	Asset Development	-.199	-3.545	.000	1.507
	Admn Monitor Control	.312	4.488	.000	2.302
	Social Justice	.541	7.813	.000	2.288
	Environment Development	.178	3.723	.000	1.088
	Public Health Service	-.015	-.297	.767	1.221

District 4

Model		Standardized Coefficients	t	Sig.	
		Beta			VIF
1	(Constant)	-.220	-.579	.563	
	Asset Development	-.081	-1.168	.244	2.051
	Admn Monitor Control	.276	3.789	.000	2.266
	Social Justice	.538	7.452	.000	2.231
	Environment Development	.192	3.836	.000	1.075
	Public Health Service	-.089	-1.491	.137	1.519

District 5

Model		Standardized Coefficients	t	Sig.	
		Beta			VIF
1	(Constant)	-.627	-1.742	.083	
	Asset Development	-.124	-2.000	.047	1.974
	Admn Monitor Control	.269	3.954	.000	2.366
	Social Justice	.569	8.148	.000	2.504
	Environment Development	.159	3.383	.001	1.132
	Public Health Service	.013	.244	.808	1.505

District 6

Model		Standardized Coefficients	t	Sig.	
		Beta			VIF
1	(Constant)	-.625	-1.717	.088	
	Asset Development	-.099	-1.564	.119	2.058
	Admn Monitor Control	.264	3.846	.000	2.406
	Social Justice	.587	8.350	.000	2.526
	Environment Development	.136	2.896	.004	1.122
	Public Health Service	-.020	-.352	.725	1.607

District 7

Model		Standardized Coefficients Beta	t	Sig.	VIF
1	(Constant)	.040	.107	.915	
	Asset Development	.072	.926	.356	2.546
	Admn Monitor Control	.257	3.493	.001	2.310
	Social Justice	.511	6.886	.000	2.354
	Environment Development	.142	2.821	.005	1.084
	Public Health Service	-.165	-2.565	.011	1.763

District 8

Model		Standardized Coefficients Beta	t	Sig.	VIF
1	(Constant)	-.509	-1.412	.160	
	Asset Development	-.208	-3.840	.000	1.591
	Admn Monitor Control	.328	4.880	.000	2.445
	Social Justice	.554	8.211	.000	2.464
	Environment Development	.150	3.315	.001	1.108
	Public Health Service	.021	.425	.671	1.265

Over all Tripura

Model		Standardized Coefficients Beta	t	Sig.	VIF
1	(Constant)	-.485	-3.760	.000	
	Asset Development	-.137	-6.347	.000	1.856
	Admn Monitor Control	.294	12.064	.000	2.357
	Social Justice	.556	22.616	.000	2.396
	Environment Development	.170	10.236	.000	1.100
	Public Health Service	-.034	-1.785	.074	1.429

Table-7: District wise Regression Coefficient Tables

Therefore from the above tables, the insignificant co-efficient values could be identified, and they should be removed while developing the revised regression equation. Public Health Service is found to be insignificant ($p<0.05$). Moreover, the Variance Inflation Factor (VIF) score is less than 4 which indicates that there are no multicollinearity issues associated with the dataset. Further, the low correlation among the independent variables evident from the Pearson's correlation coefficients identifies with the fact that the independent variables are truly independent and there is limited scope for multicollinearity.

Therefore from the above table, we develop the revised regression equation which is as below;

Rural Livelihood Development = -0.485 – 137 Asset Development + 0.297 Administrative Monitoring & Control + 0.556 Social Justice + 0.170 Environment Development

From the above equation of the overall Tripura, we can conclude that,

H1. There is a significant positive relationship between the development of Rural Livelihood and Asset Build Up at the Macro level. **(Accepted)**

H2. Development of Rural Livelihood has a positive association with Administrative Monitoring & Control. **(Accepted)**

H3. Development of Rural Livelihood is significantly and positively associated with social justice. **(Accepted)**

H4. Development of Rural Livelihood and Environmental Development are significantly associated. **(Accepted)**

H5. There is a significant positive relationship between the development of Rural Livelihood and the public health care system. **(Rejected)**

(Note: However, in one district the regression co-efficient value has been found to be significant)

Correlations (N= 1602)

		Livelihood Development	Asset Development	Admin Monitor Control	Social Justice	Environment Development	Public Health Service
Pearson Correlation	Livelihood Development	1.000	.368	.652	.723	.378	.274
	Asset Development		1.000	.584	.575	.187	.517
	Admn Monitor Control			1.000	.728	.278	.385
	Social Justice				1.000	.280	.444
	Environment Development					1.000	.112
	Public Health Service						1.000

Table 8 : Correlation among the variables

	West Tripura	District 2	District 3	District 4	District 5	District 6	District 7	District 8	Tripura State
(Constant)	-.358	-.404	-.403	-.220	-.627	-.625	.040	-.509	-.485
Asset Development	-.114	-.207	-.199	-.081	-.124	-.099	.072	-.208	-.137
Administrative Monitoring & Control	.286	.324	.312	.276	.269	.264	.257	.328	.294
Social Justice	.546	.539	.541	.538	.569	.587	.511	.554	.556
Environment Development	.185	.171	.178	.192	.159	.136	.142	.150	.170
Public Health Service	-.056	-.015	-.015	-.089	.013	-.020	-.165	.021	-.034

Table-9: Regression Co-efficient Table

However, it is important to note that the study has found IV3 i.e., Social Justice is the most important predictor (62%) while IV2 i.e., Administrative Monitoring & Control (18%) and Environment Development (12.9%) are the second and third important predictors. Therefore we can conclude that MGNREGA is working steadfastly not only in the field of rural livelihood development but at the same time it is working as a powerful instrument in providing people social justice and causing the development of the overall environment.

Coefficients
Target: Livelihood Development

Model Term	Coefficient ▶	Sig.	Importance
Intercept	-0.489	.000	
IV3_N_transformed	0.898	.000	0.624
IV2_N_transformed	0.347	.000	0.181
IV4_N_transformed	0.186	.000	0.129
IV1_N_transformed	-0.192	.000	0.062
IV5_N_transformed	-0.028	.045	0.005

Table-10: Predictor's Importance

7

Discussions

The proposed model identified the five crucial parameters influencing livelihood development for the rural folk: Asset Development (A&D), Administrative Monitoring & Control, Social Justice, Environment Development and Public Health Care System. The study reveals that the Public Health Care System at the ground level across all districts of Tripura needs significant up-gradation as the people at the bottom of the pyramid are in dire need of healthcare facilities, particularly in remote areas. This finding is in sync with the NITI Aayog's report of 2019 wherein Tripura is placed at the moderately improved state in terms of incremental performance in health care services among the smaller states of India.

The main objective of MGNERGA is to create assets with respect to the community as well as at the individual level. However, the study finds that there is a lacuna in the formation of assets at these levels as it contributes merely 6.2% in the predictor's importance table, thus causing a negative impact on livelihood development. The finding of the study corroborates Tripura's rank at the national level in terms of the creation of jobs (ranked at 8th position with an unemployment rate of 20% as of May 2021).

The study finds that influence social justice has been very strong in the society which is visible through the practice of intervention of Ombudsman in appropriate situations, women participation and inertia of wage administration, successful prevention of seasonal migration, enhancement of social skills among women beneficiaries, enhancement of Local Government Units (LGUs) and availability of LGU representatives.

Another important finding of the study is the identification of administrative monitoring and control as the backbone of MGNERGA, which helps to accelerate the implementation process of this flagship programme. This variable exerts a strong influence over rural livelihood by ensuring the requisite administrative control over the works done through the scheme. Enhancement of community participation, social participation of women, participation of people in Social Audit, participation of the disadvantaged groups, low-status groups, minority groups and poorer groups in community programmes, enforcement of Rule of Law, transparency in the MGNREGA work processes, increasing efficiency through capacity building, expansion of economic activities leading to increased participation of women in the decision-making process, maintaining equity, reduction of indebtedness, improvement of food and non-food consumption levels, enhancement of the rate of grievance redressal, and reduction in the number of false redressal issues received have collectively contributed in measuring the administrative monitoring and control.

Tripura has observed a strong impact of MGNREGS implementation on the environment. This study corroborates the potential and positive impact of the actions taken under the scheme to reflect a sustainable environment which can be measured by the factors like, increase in the number of trees/roadside plantation activities, enhancement in the number of ponds, improvement of the drainage system, increasing number of VATs /Pits for garbage disposal and avoid littering.

7.1. Recommendations

The study would like torecommend that the following improvement areas where the policymakers must concentrate to realize the underlying objective of the MGNREGS. The improvement areas are as follows;

1. Development of roads
2. Improvement of availability of drinking water
3. Improvement of sanitation system
4. Improvement of sanitation facilities
5. Improvement of irrigation system
6. Improvement of water conservation activities like restoration of water bodies, rainwater conservation etc.
7. Improvement of watershed management.

Further, it is also recommended that the health care facilities should be fostered to provide the best services to the rural poor. The specific improvement areas are as follows;

1. Improvement of public health services and increase in the number of public health centers,
2. Increase in the number of Doctors in PHCs and CHCs,
3. Improve family hygiene,
4. Improvement of environment hygiene,
5. Increase in the number of Nurses and other health staff in PHCs and CH,
6. Increase in the number of medical shops,
7. Improvement in the availability of medicines in local hospitals,
8. Availability of minimum clinical test facility in local hospitals,
9. Improvement of overall health condition of the family.

Annexures

Annexure-1:

Block wise GRS who attended in the Focused Group Discussion (FGD)

SL.No	Name	District	Block
1.	Pijush Bose	Gomati	Amarpur Rd Block
2.	Matilal Dutta	West Tripura	Lefunga Rd Block
3.	Bijoy Rudra Paul	West Tripura	Dukli Rd Block
4.	Sujit Paul	West Tripura	Mohanpur Rd Block
5.	Bikram Das	West Tripura	Lembucherra, Bamutia Rd Block
6.	Subrata Das	West Tripura	Old Agartala Rd Block
7.	Santosh Debbarma	West Tripura	Belbari Rd Block
8.	Tapan Kumar Singha Barman	Dhalai	Durgachowmuhani Rd Block
9.	Subinoy Paul	Dhalai	Salema Rd Block
10.	Debapratap Ghosh	Dhalai	Ambassa Rd Block
11.	Sanjit Reang	Dhalai	Dumburnagar Rd Block
12.	Pravat Tripura	Dhalai	Manu Rd Block
13.	Uttam Das	South Tripura	Satchand Rd Block
14.	Tamal Kanti Ghosh	South Tripura	Jolaibari Rd Block
15.	Sankar Das	South Tripura	Rupaichari Rd Block
16.	Dipak Das	South Tripura	Bharath Chandra Nagar Rd Block
17.	Samir Paul	South Tripura	Hrishyamukh Rd Block
18.	Partha Das	South Tripura	Rajnagar Rd Block
19.	Swapan Kumar Deb	Sepahijala	Bishalgarh Rd Block
20.	Binoy Debbarma	Sepahijala	Jampuijala Rd Block
21.	Kartik Kumar Debbarma	Sepahijala	Nalchar Rd Block
22.	Basudeb Banik	Sepahijala	Kathalia Rd Block
23.	Prabal Kar	Sepahijala	Sepahijala Rd Block
24.	Haridas Sarkar	Sepahijala	Boxanagar Rd Block
25.	Biswajit Dutta	Sepahijala	Charilam Rd Block

26.	Ajoy Malakar	Unakoti	Chandipur Rd Block
27.	Sanjoy Singha	Unakoti	Kumarghat Rd Block
28.	Sanjib Singha	Unakoti	Kumarghat Rd Block
29.	Uttam Gope	Khowai	Khowai Rd Block
30.	Biswajit Bhowmik	Khowai	Kalyanpur Rd Block
31.	Subhash Debbarma	Khowai	Padmabil Rd Block
32.	Dinesh Debnath	North Tripura	Laljuri Rd Block
33.	Md. Montar Ali	North Tripura	Kalacherra Rd Block
34.	Nirmal Nama	North Tripura	Kadamtala Rd Block
35.	Md. Jaydul Hussain	North Tripura	Jubarajnagar Rd Block
36.	Jayanta Debnath	North Tripura	Panisagar Rd Block

Annexure-2

List of Pradhans in West Tripura District

Block	Gram Panchayat	Name of Pradhan/ V.P
Bamutia	Ananganagar	Kartik Biswas
	Bhagalpur	Basana Das
	Debendranagar	Rupasi Das (Kal)
	Dighalia	Dipak Bin
	Laxmilunga	Aparna Das
	Nabagram	Shampa Deb (Sen)
	Narsingarh	Nibedita Das (Saha)
	Nutannagar	Anita Acharjee (Biswas)
	Paschim Gandhigram	Suniti Sarkar
	Patunagar	Mintu Lal Saha
	Singerbil	Puspa Tanti
	Uttar Lembucherra	Gouranga Sarkar
Dukli	Anandanagar	Shila Banik
	Bagmara	Pampa Das Debnath
	Ballabpur	Milan Das (Roy)
	Bikramnagar	Jaba Sundari Paul (Deb)
	Chowmuhani Bazar	Manik Sarkar
	Dukli	Rajyashri Chowdhury
	Fultali	Kajal Rani Das
	I C Nagar	Sita Rani Sarkar
	Kanchanmala	Pradip Kumar Majumder
	Kathaltali	Puja Podder (Singha)
	Khash Madhupur	Rinki Das
	Madhuban	Bakul Rani Nama
	Maheshkhola	Swapan Das
	Malaynagar	Sandhya Rani Malakar (Das)
	Pandabpur	Gouri Das
	Paschim Anandanagar	Sukumar Sarkar

	Sekerkote	Dipti Dey
	Srinagar	Bhajan Paul
	Suryamaninagar	Biva Sarkar Das
Jirania	Barjala Binapani	Nanda Ram Debbarma
	Durganagar	Ratan R. Paul
	Harijoy Chow Para	Shaibya Debnath
	Kobrakhamar	Bishu Debbarma
	Krishnanagar	Moni Das Baishnab
	Majlishpur	Mousumi Das
	Paschim Majlishpur	Sanjit Debnath
	Purba Barjala	Rupali Das
	Sachindranagar	Karuna Goswami (Sharma)
	Uttar Majlishpur	Beauti Das
Mohanpur	Bijoynagar	Sanjib Sarkar
	Brahmakunda	Nakul Santal
	Gajaria	Subhash Sarkar
	Harina Khola	Sefali Kanda
	Ishanpur	Lipika Das
	Kalacherra	Aparna Sutradhar
	Kamalghat	Soma Sarkar
	Mohinipur	Rama Deb
	Paschim Fatikcherra	Dipankar Das
	Paschim Kamalghat	Amita Debbarma
	Rangachara	Rita Gour
	Simna	Biplab Deb
Old Agartala	Debram Thakur	Bijoy Sarkar
	Madhya Champamura	Bikash Shil
	Paschim Champamura	Sheuli Sarkar
	Paschim Noabadi	Sabita Mallik
	Paschim Noagaon	Jaya Debnath
	Purba Noagaon	Manoranjan Debnath
	Radha Kishore Nagar	Gopa Das
	Tulakona	Ashutosh Lodh
	Uttar Champamura	Anima Das

Annexure -3

List of Pradhans in Gomati District

Block	Gram Panchayat	Name of The Resource Person
Amarpur	Birganj	Purnima Das
	Debbari	Suchitra Das
	Mailak	Sampa Das
	Paschim Dalak	Gopal Sarkar
	Paschim Malbasa	Shilpi Das
	Purba Rangamati	Maran Ch. Ghosh
	Rangamati	Bulti Das (Majumder)
	Rangkang	Sadhana Roy (Das)
	Thakcherra	Rakesh Das
	Gram Panchayat	**Name of The Resource Person**
Kakraban	Dakshin Mirza	Shyamal Debnath
	Dushpuskarini	Phanindra Kr. Debnath
	Gangachara	Sibaprasad Sen
	Hurijal	Md. Bahar Miah
	Kakraban	Ratna Sutradhar (Das)
	Mirza	Prabir Majumder
	Murapara	Dilip Barman
	Palatana	Sabita Das (Nama)
	Purba Mirza	Sadhan Debnath
	Purba Palatana	Sumita Rani Nama (Sarkar)
	Rani	Aghor Jamatia
	Shilghati	Rakhi Sarkar (Mitra)
	Tulamura	Litan Paul
	Uttar Tulamura	Shikha Rani Shil (Shom)
Matabari	Chandrapur Colony	Rina Ghosh
	Chandrapur R.F.	Ram Kr. Reang
	Chandrapur Village	Nantu Laskar
	Dakshin Maharani	Mantu Ch. Das
	Dakshin Murapara	Madan Gopal Baidya

	Garjeechara	Prantosh Das
	Holakhet	Aparna Das (Dey)
	Jowalikhamar	Lakshman Debnath
	Kunjaban	Champa Das
	Laxmipati	Ashu Rani Das
	Maharani	Shapan Ch. Das
	Matabari	Jhulan Das
	Paschim Khilpara	Shikha Das
	Pitra	Sima Rani Das
	Potamati	Anjana Debnath
	Purba Kunjaban	Laxmi Shil (Saha)
	Rajnagar	Priti Sarkar
	Uttar Chandrapur	Anita Debnath
	Uttar Kalaban	Gulam Noatia
	Uttar Maharani	Nani Gopal Debnath
Tepania	Amtali	Litan Debnath
	Bagabasa	Karuna Debnath
	Barabhiya	Abhijit Majumder
	Dakshin Bagma	Nimai Das
	Dhajanagar	Bapi Ch. Dey
	Gakulpur	Mrinal Das
	Garjanmura	Anima Ghosh
	Hadra	Laxmi Dey (Majumder)
	Karaiyamura	Anupam Ghosh
	Paschim Dhajanagar	Amita Sutradhar
	Purba Barabhaiya	Minu Rani Paul
	Purba Dhajanagar	Pradip Debnath
	Purba Gakulpur	Puspa Das
	Rangamati	Dali Das (Majumder)
	Shalghara	Thakur Das Sarkar
	Tepania	Anita Mallik (Goswami)
	Uttar Shalgarah	Laxmi Shil

Annexure -4

List of Pradhans in South District

Block	Gram Panchayat	Name of the Resource Person
Bharat Chandra Nagar	Chittamara	Brighu Rani Tripura
	Dakshin Bharat Chandra Nagar	Pradip Majumder
	Ishan Ch. Nagar	Kamal Majumder
	Paschim Kalabaria	Sujata Neogi (Dey)
	Paschim Paikhola	Haradhan Mallik
	Purba Kalabaria	Saradindu Majumder
	Purba Piparikhola	Maya Rani Das
	Sukanta Nagar	Tapan Guha
	Uttar Bharat Chandra Nagar	Tanima Baidya
Bokafa	Bokafa	Nirmal Reang
	Betaga	Pradip Debnath
	Gardhang	Debashish Das
	Kachannagar	Rita Mog
	Lowgang	Rakhi Majumder (Das)
	Paschim Kathalia	Kabita Debbarma (Gurum)
	Radhakishore Ganj	Jahar Lal Debnath
	Subhash Colony	Dilip Bepari
Jolaibari	Charakbai	Kakali Paul Nandi
	Debdaru	Abaitu Mog
	Madhya Pillak	Ratan Baidya
	Paschim Charakbai	Sadhan Das
	Paschim Jolaibari	Iva Datta
	Purba Charakbai	Ganaraj Pal
	Swadeshnagar	Ashish Das
	Thakurcharra	Thaichau Mog
Poangbari	Amlighat	Gobinda Das
	Dakshin Srinagar	Manju Sarkar

	Krishnanagar	Ujjwali Mahajan (Majumder)
	Madhabnagar	Kartik Das
	Rajnagar	Ratan Majumder
	Srinagar	Kali Sankar Datta
Rajnagar	Dakshin Radhanagar	Anjali Barman
	Dakshin Rajnagar	Sumati Sarkar (Das)
	Dakshin Srirampur	Krishnadhan Shil
	Durgapur	Jugal Ch. Sarkar
	Ekinpur	Renu Majumder
	Gouranga Bazar	Pradip Dutta
	Indira Nagar	Malati Sarkar (Debnath)
	Jashmura	Guneswary Reang
	Nihar Nagar	Nirmal Kumar Tripura
	Paschim Pipariakhola	Anima Shil Sharma
	Radhanagar	Machaching Mog (Sarkar)
	Rajnagar	Bebi Das
	Uttar Rangamura	Simal Ch. Das
Satchand	Battala	Dipak Majumder
	Brajendranagar	Sati Bhowmik
	Dakshin Bhuratali	Bipul Debnath
	Damdama	Ranjit Singha
	Doulbari	Sadhan Chandra Nath
	Guachand Nandigram	Dipali Dey (Basu)
	Kalachara	Sunil Kanti Tripura
	Kalapania	Manik Roy
	Magurchara	Krishna Nandi
	Manubazar	Apu Bhowmik
	Nabagram	Tapasi Sarkar
	Paschim Harina	Narayan Chandra Debnath
	Paschim Zelefa	Susmita Majumder
	Paschim Sabroom	Tumpa Sarkar (Das)
	Purba Harina	Anima Das
	Purba Zelefa	Bandana Das

	Rajib Nagar	Chandan Debnath
	Satchand	Ratna Das
	Sukanta Palli	Goutam Das
	Thaibong	Bhabaranjan Nath
	Uttar Bhuratali	Pranayan Das
	V.K. Palli	Shiuli Roy

Annexure -5

List of Pradhans in Sepahijala District

Block	Gram Panchayat	Name of the Resource Person
Bishalgarh	Arabindanagar	Mira Debnath
	Badhyardighi	Ratnasuku Das
	Bhati Lama	Mira Shil
	Bhatibari	Swapan Debbarma
	Champamura	Ashtami Das
	Chandranagar	Sabita Roy Sarkar
	Dakshin Madhupur	Kalyan Nama
	Devipur	Ashim Sarkar
	Gajaria	Sabita Das
	Ganiamara	Sanjoy Dasgupta
	Golaghati	Nishikanta Shil
	Gopinagar	Sanju Nama
	Harishnagar	Akhi Modi (Sutradhar)
	K.K. Nagar	Anamika Das (Biswas)
	Kaiyadepha	Chandana Sarkar
	Kamalasagar	Chandan Sarkar
	Kasba	Prantosh Shil
	Konaban	Rupali Dutta
	Laxmibill	Pinki Saha (Dutta)
	Lembutali	Maya Rani Debbarma
	Madhya Laxmibill	Manik Das
	N.C. Nagar	Pranati Biswas (Das)
	Nabinagar	Laxmi Das
	Pathalia	Anita Das (Deb)
	Pathariadwar	Anjali Roy
	Prabhurampur	Mina Laskar
	Purathal Rajnagar	Suparna Majumder
	Purba Gakulnagar	Papia Das (Biswas)
	Radhanagar	Ratna Sarkar
	Raghunathpur	Ripa Choudhury Das

Boxanagar	Anandanagar	Abdul Haque
	Bagber	Sukhen Ch. Das
	Boxanagar	Niranjan Nama
	Dakshin Kalamchora	Jayanti Rani Sarkar
	Durgapur	Abdul Sattar
	Kalashimura	Joyasree Sarkar (Das)
	Mainama	Muslem Miah Bhuiya
	Matinagar	Rina Biswas (Das)
	Nabadwip Chandra Nagar	Amimaner Nesha
	Uttar Kalamchora	Sabitri Das
	Valuarchar	Anil Ch. Das
Charilam	Aralia	Saptam Sarkar
	Barjala	Bhagyashree Debnath
	Bishramganj	Sudhangshu Das Baishnab
	Brajapur	Mithu Deb
	Chesrimai	Pradip Debnath
	Dakshin Charilam	Jhunu Datta
	Lal Singmura	Soma Debnath
	Madhya Brajapur	Shikha Das
	Ramcherra	Shyamal Debnath
	Uttar Charilam	Anjana Sarkar (Das)
	Uttar Brajapur	Moni Debnath
Kathalia	Bashpukur	Maran Sutradhar
	Bejimara	Pran Krishna Bhowmik
	Bhabanipur	Krishnadhan Debnath
	Dakshin Maheshpur	Mumpi Dutta Deb
	Dakshin Paharpur	Babul Ch. Dhar
	Dhanpur	Sukumar Debnath
	Jatrapur	Rina Rani Paul
	Kalapania	Anwar Hussian
	Kali Krishna Nagar	Subhash Ch. Pal

	Kathalia	Bijuli Bhowmik
	Manarchak	Ratna Rani Das
	Nidaya	Bhanu Rani Paul
	Nirvoypur	Bipul Majumder
	Rabindranagar	Priyanka Sarkar
	Sonapur	Minu Begam
	Sovapur	Sukla Banerjee
	Srimantapur	Mursheda Begam
	Uttar Maheshpur	Tanusree Pal
Mohanbhog	Kalamkhet	Manika Das
	Kamrangatali	Prava Debnath
	Mohanbhog	Purnima Nandi
	Purba Chandighar	Rupa Sarkar (Nama)
	Telkajla	Suman Ghosh
Nalchar	Bardowal	Rita Das
	Chandanmura	Anjali Das
	Dakshin Nalchar	Briti Sundar Sarkar
	Khascchowmohani	Rajib Sarkar
	Khedabari	Jhunu Chandra Das
	Kumariakucha	Mousumi Das
	Laxmendhepa	Sajal Debnath
	Purba Durlovnarayan	Nabina Das
	Purba Nalchar	Sathi Das
	Paschim Nalchar	Ratna Majumder (Das)
	Poangbari	Dipali Sarkar
	Rangamati	Karunbala Sarkar (Das)
	Shibnagar	Sukumar Ghosh
	Taxapara	Beauti Bhowmik (Das)

Annexure-6

List of Pradhans in North Tripura District

District	Block	Name of (Gp)/(Vc)	GP/VC
North Tripura	Damcherra	Damcherra	VC
		Damcgerra R.F	VC
		Hingskang	VC
		Juri R.F	VC
		Kacharicherra	VC
		Kalagang Sarkhi	VC
		Khedacherra	VC
		Monacherra	VC
		Piplacherra	VC
		Rahumcherra	VC
		Thumsarai Para	VC
		Uttamjoy Para	VC
		West Damcherra	VC
	Dasda	Anandasagar	GP
		Daincherra	GP
		Dakshin Tuisama	VC
		Dasamanipara	GP
		Gachirampara	VC
		Kalapani	GP
		Kangrai	VC
		Khakchangpara	VC
		Khumpui	VC
		Manuchailengta	GP
		Paschim Bhandarima	GP
		Purba Satnala	GP
		Radhamadhavpur	GP
		S.K. Sherhmun	GP

North Tripura		Subhashnagar	GP
		Uttar Dasda	GP
		Uttar Tuisama	VC
	Jampui Hills	Kalagang	VC
		Kanpui	VC
		Longaivalley	VC
		Paschim Hmunpui	VC
		Sabual	VC
		Tlangsang	VC
		Vanghmun	VC
	Jubaraj Nagar	Bagbasa	GP
		Balidhum	GP
		Charupasa	GP
		Dewanpasa	GP
		Dhupirbond	GP
		Huplong	GP
		Jubarajnagar	GP
		Kameswar	GP
		Lal Cherra	GP
		Madhuban	GP
		Mangalkhali	GP
		North Ganganagar	GP
		Paschim Dewanpasha	GP
		Paschim Tilthai	GP
		Purba Tilthai	GP
		Radhapur	GP
		Rajnagar	GP
		South Ganganagar	GP
		Sripur	GP
		Tongibari	GP
		Uptakhali	GP
		Zaithang	VC
	Kadamtala	Baghan	GP
		Bargul	GP
		Bishnupur	GP

North Tripura		Brajendranagar	GP
		Churaibari	GP
		Dakshin Kadamtala	GP
		Fulbari	GP
		Kadamtala	GP
		Kalagangerpar	GP
		Kurti	GP
		Purba Churaibari	GP
		Purba Fulbari	GP
		Rajnagar	GP
		Ranibari	GP
		Sarala	GP
		Saraspur	GP
		Satsangam	GP
		Tarakpur	GP
		Uttar Fulbari	GP
	Kalacherra	Algapur	GP
		Balicherra	GP
		Baruakandi	GP
		Bhagyapur	GP
		Chndrapur	GP
		East Hurua	GP
		Gobindapur	GP
		Ichai Lalcherra	GP
		Laxminagar	GP
	Kalacherra	Nadiapur Sanichara	GP
		North Hurua	GP
		Pratyekroy	GP
		Raghna	GP
		Sakaibari	GP
		Sanicherra	GP
		South Hurua	GP
		West Ichailalcherra	GP

North Tripura	Laljuri	Chandipur	GP
		Dakshin Laljuri	GP
		Jamaraipara	VC
		Joymani Para	VC
		Kanchancherra	GP
		Kanchanpur	GP
		Makumcherra	VC
		Rabindranagar	GP
		Salkaham	VC
		Santipur	GP
		Shibnagar	GP
		Ujan Machmara	GP
		Uttar Laljuri	GP
	Panisagar	Agnipasa	GP
		Bilthai	GP
		Chandra Halam Para	VC
		Dakshin Padmabil	GP
		Dakshin Panisagar	GP
		Deocherra	GP
		Indurail	GP
		Jalabasa	GP
		Noagang	GP
		Paschim Padmabil	GP
		Pekucherra	GP
		Purba Jalabasa	GP
		Purba Rowa	VC
		Ramnagar	GP
		Rowa	VC
		Uttar Deocherra	GP
		Uttar Padmabil	GP
		West Panisagar	GP

Annexure -7

List of Pradhans in Unokoti District

District	Block	Name of (Gp)/ (Vc)	GP/VC
Unakoti	Chandipur	Bilashpur	GP
		Birchandranagar	GP
		Chandipur	GP
		Chantail	GP
		Dhanbilash	GP
		Fultali	GP
		Golokpur	VC
		Halairpar	GP
		Jamtailbari	VC
		Jarultali	GP
		Manu Valley	GP
		Milong	VC
		Murticherra	GP
		Rangrung	GP
		Samrurpar	GP
		Singirbil	VC
		Sorojini	GP
		Srirampur	GP
	Gournagar	Bhagabannagar	GP
		Deoracherra	VC
		Dhaliarkandi	GP
		East Yeajakawra	GP
		Fulbarikandi	GP
		Goldharpur	GP
		Gournagar	GP
		Hiracherra	VC
		Ichabpur	GP
		Irani	GP

Unakoti		Jalai	GP
		Jubarajnagar	GP
		Kaulikura	GP
		Khowrabil	GP
		Latiapura	GP
		Laxmipur	GP
		Maguruli	GP
		Noorpur	GP
		Rangauti	GP
		Srinathpur	GP
		Tillagaon	GP
		Unakoti	VC
		Yeazekhawra	GP
	Kumarghat	Ambedkar Nagar	GP
		Betcherra	GP
		Dakshin Unakoti	VC
		Darchawi	VC
		Demdum	VC
		Deo-Velly	VC
		Dudpur	GP
		East Kanchanbari	GP
		East Raitwisa	VC
		East Ratacherra	GP
		Fatikcherra Dasarath Deb	VC
		Fatikroy	GP
		Gakulnagar	GP
		Ganganagar	GP
		Jagannathpur	GP
		Juricherra	VC
		Kanchanbari	GP
		Krishnanagar	GP
		Laljuri	GP
		Masauli	GP
		Radhanagar	GP
		Rajkandi	VC

Unakoti		Rajnagar	GP
		Ratiabari	GP
		Saidacherra	VC
		Saidarpar	GP
		Sonaimuri	GP
		Sukanta Nagar	GP
		Taraninagar	GP
		Ujandudpur	GP
		Vidyasagar	GP
		West Kanchanbari	GP
		West Masauli	GP
		West Ratacherra	GP
	Pencharthal	Andharcherra	VC
		Bagaicherra	VC
		Dakshin Dhanicherra	VC
		Dakshin Machmara	VC
		Karaicherra	VC
		Machamara	VC
		Nabincherra	VC
		Nalkata	VC
		Pencharthal	VC
		Purba Andharcherra	VC
		Ramguna	VC
		Shantipur	VC
		Solonala	VC
		Sonarampara	VC
		Uttar Dhanicherra	VC
		Uttar Machmara	VC

Annexure -8

Photo

Gallery of Focus Group Discussion

Annexure -9

Photo

Glimpses of the District Wise Programmes Conducted

Gallery from West Tripura District

Gallery from West Tripura District

Gallery from Gomati District

Gallery from Gomati District

Gallery from South Tripura District

Gallery from North Tripura District

Gallery from Unokoti District

Annexure –10

Glimpses of the Micro Level Data Collection

Data Collection at Gandacherra Viilage

Collection at Chawmanu Collection at Chandipur

Data collection at Rowa Village

Collection at Chawmanu Collection at Chandipur

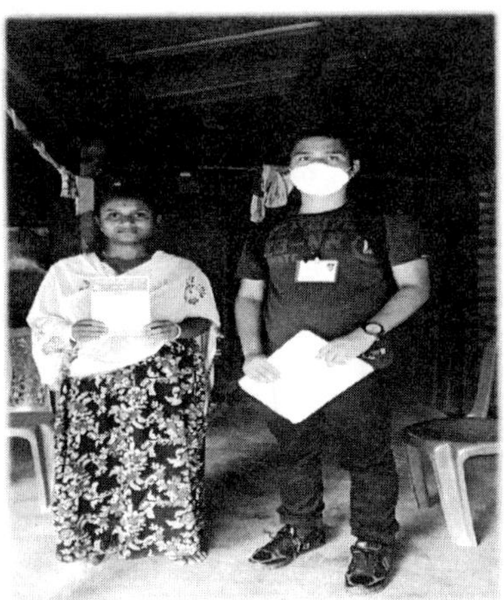

Collection at Amarpur

Collection at Bagaicherra

Annexure -11

Questionnaire for Micro Level Data Survey
Project Title: Impact of Mahatma Gandhi NREGA on Development of Rural Livelihood
Funded By :ICSSR, New Delhi

Name of the Respondent:..

Name of the Village:..

Mobile Number:...

A. Demographic Profile of the Respondent:

Sl. No.	Age	Gender (M/F)	Educa-tional Status	Home stead Land (kani/ gonda)	Agri. Land (kani/go-nad)	Agricul-ture Produc-tion (Rs.)	Job card Num-ber	Type of dwelling (kaccha /pacca)	Asset build up (if any)	Occupation		Income (Rs.)	
										Pri-mary	Second-ary	Pri-mary	Sec-ondary

B. Opinion of the Respondent:

Sr. No.	Degree of Opinion / Statements	Strongly Disagree	Disagree	Disagree Somewhat	Undecided	Agree Somewhat	Agree	Strongly Agree	Remarks
		1	2	3	4	5	6	7	
1.	The MGNREG activities has helped in enhancement of income level(RLDIL)	1	2	3	4	5	6	7	
2.	The MGNREG activities has helped in improvement of land productivity/ plantation/ horticulture activities/ sericulture activities/ fishery activities/ agricultural production (RLDABC)	1	2	3	4	5	6	7	
3.	The MGNREG activities has helped in land labeling. (RLDABC)	1	2	3	4	5	6	7	
4.	The MGNREG activities has helped in family education. (RLDSS)	1	2	3	4	5	6	7	
5.	The MGNREG activities has helped in improvement of social awareness (RLDSS)	1	2	3	4	5	6	7	
6.	The MGNREG activities has helped in improvement of community relationship. (RLDSS)	1	2	3	4	5	6	7	
Independent Variable 1 : Asset Development									

Sr. No.	Degree of Opinion / Statements	Strongly Disagree	Disagree	Disagree Somewhat	Unde-cided	Agree Some-what	Agree	Strongly Agree	Remarks
		1	2	3	4	5	6	7	
7.	The MGNREG activities has helped in development of roads(RLDAAD)	1	2	3	4	5	6	7	
8.	The MGNREG activities has helped in improvement of availability of drinking water(RLDAAD)	1	2	3	4	5	6	7	
9.	The MGNREG activities has helped in improvement of sanitation system (RLDAAD)	1	2	3	4	5	6	7	
10.	The MGNREG activities has helped in improvement in availability of sanitation facilities(RLDAAD)	1	2	3	4	5	6	7	
11.	The MGNREG activities has helped in improvement of irrigation system(RLDAAD)	1	2	3	4	5	6	7	
12.	The MGNREG activities has helped in improvement of water conservation activities like restoration of water bodies, rainwater conservation etc(RLDAAD)	1	2	3	4	5	6	7	
13.	The MGNREG activities has helped inwatershed management (RLDAAD)	1	2	3	4	5	6	7	
14.	The MGNREG activities has helped in improvement in afforestation and plantation activities (RLDAAD)	1	2	3	4	5	6	7	

Sr. No.	Degree of Opinion / Statements	Strongly Disagree	Disagree	Disagree Somewhat	Undecided	Agree Somewhat	Agree	Strongly Agree	Remarks
		1	2	3	4	5	6	7	
Independent Variable 2: Administrative Monitoring and Control (AMC)									
15.	The MGNREG activities has helped in enhancement of community participation (RLDAMC)	1	2	3	4	5	6	7	
16.	The MGNREG activities has helped to increase the level the social participation of women. (RLDAMC)	1	2	3	4	5	6	7	
17.	The MGNREG activities has helped to increase in the level the participation of people in Social Audit processes (RLDAMC)	1	2	3	4	5	6	7	
18.	The MGNREG activities has helped to increase the level the participation of the disadvantaged groups, low status groups, minority groups and poorer groups in such community programmes and participatory processes (RLDAMC)	1	2	3	4	5	6	7	
19.	The MGNREG activities has helped in enforcement of Rule of Law (RLDAMC)	1	2	3	4	5	6	7	

Sr. No.	Degree of Opinion / Statements	Strongly Disagree	Disagree	Disagree Somewhat	Undecided	Agree Somewhat	Agree	Strongly Agree	Remarks
		1	2	3	4	5	6	7	
20.	The MGNREG activities has helped in maintaining transparency in the MGNREGA work processes (RLDAMC)	1	2	3	4	5	6	7	
21.	The MGNREG activities has helped in increasing efficiency through capacity building(RLDAMC)								
22.	The MGNREG activities has helped in expansion of economic activities leading to increased participation of women in decision making process(RLDAMC)	1	2	3	4	5	6	7	
23.	The MGNREG activities has helped in maintaining equity (RLDAMC)	1	2	3	4	5	6	7	
24.	The MGNREG activities has helped in reduction of indebtedness (RLDAMC)	1	2	3	4	5	6	7	
25.	The MGNREG activities has helped in improvement of food and non-food consumption levels (RLDAMC)	1	2	3	4	5	6	7	
26.	The MGNREG activities has helped in enhancement of rate of grievance redressal (RLDAMC).	1	2	3	4	5	6	7	

Sr. No.	Degree of Opinion / Statements	Strongly Disagree	Disagree	Disagree Somewhat	Undecided	Agree Somewhat	Agree	Strongly Agree	Remarks
		1	2	3	4	5	6	7	
27.	The MGNREG activities has helped in reduction in the number of false redressal issues received. (RLDAMC).	1	2	3	4	5	6	7	
Independent Variable 3 : Social Justice									
28.	The MGNREG activities has helped in making the Ombudsman proactive. (RLDSJ).	1	2	3	4	5	6	7	
29.	The MGNREG activities has helped in improving the women wage rate/inertia of wage administration (RLDSJ).	1	2	3	4	5	6	7	
30.	The MGNREG activities has helped in improving gender relations. (RLDSJ).	1	2	3	4	5	6	7	
31.	The govt. support at micro level through MGNREGA towards development of rural livelihood has helped in checking seasonal migration (RLDSJ).	1	2	3	4	5	6	7	
32.	The MGNREG activities has helped in enhancement of Social Skills among women workers. (RLDSJ).	1	2	3	4	5	6	7	
33.	The MGNREG activities has helped in enhancement of Local Govt. Units (LGUs) and availability of LGU Representatives (RLDSJ).	1	2	3	4	5	6	7	

Sr. No.	Degree of Opinion / Statements	Strongly Disagree	Disagree	Disagree Somewhat	Undecided	Agree Somewhat	Agree	Strongly Agree	Remarks
		1	2	3	4	5	6	7	
Independent Variable 4 : Environment Development									
34.	The MGNREG activities has helped in increase in the number of trees/roadside plantation activities (RLDED)	1	2	3	4	5	6	7	
35.	The MGNREG activities has helped in enhancement in number of ponds (RLDED)	1	2	3	4	5	6	7	
36.	The MGNREG activities has helped inincreasing water level in ponds (RLDED)	1	2	3	4	5	6	7	
37.	The MGNREG activities has helped in increasing number of VATs /Pits (RLDED)	1	2	3	4	5	6	7	
38.	The MGNREG activities has helped in improvement of drainage system. (RLDED)	1	2	3	4	5	6	7	
Independent Variable 5 : Public Health Services									
39.	The MGNREG activities has improved the demand for public health services/Increase in number of patients in public health centres (RLDPHS)	1	2	3	4	5	6	7	

Sr. No.	Degree of Opinion / Statements	Strongly Disagree	Disagree	Disagree Somewhat	Undecided	Agree Somewhat	Agree	Strongly Agree	Remarks
		1	2	3	4	5	6	7	
40.	The MGNREG activities has helped in increase in the number of medical shops. (RLDPHS)	1	2	3	4	5	6	7	
41.	The MGNREG activities has helped in increase in the number of Doctors in PHCs and CHCs (RLDPHS)	1	2	3	4	5	6	7	
42.	The MGNREG activities has helped in increase in the number of Nurses and other health staff in PHCs and CHCs (RLDPHS)	1	2	3	4	5	6	7	
43.	The MGNREG activities has helped to improve of family hygiene. (RLDPHS)	1	2	3	4	5	6	7	
44.	The MGNREG activities has helped in improvement of environment hygiene (RLDPHS)	1	2	3	4	5	6	7	
45.	The MGNREG activities has helped in improvement in availability of medicines in local hospitals (RLDPHS)	1	2	3	4	5	6	7	
46.	The MGNREG activities has helped in availability of minimum clinical test facility in local hospitals. (RLDPHS)	1	2	3	4	5	6	7	

Sr. No.	Degree of Opinion / Statements	Strongly Disagree	Disagree	Disagree Somewhat	Unde-cided	Agree Some-what	Agree	Strongly Agree	Remarks
		1	2	3	4	5	6	7	
47.	The MGNREG activities has helped in improvement of overall health condition of the family. (RLDPHS)	1	2	3	4	5	6	7	

Date:

Signature of the Field Investigator

Annexure-12

Questionnaire for Block/Panchayat/ADC Livelihood Survey
Conducted by CSSEIP & Department of Business Management, Tripura University
Funded by ICSSR, New Delhi

Name of the Member.................................... Mobile No...

Name of the District......................... Name of the Block...

Name of the Panchayat/ ADC Village ....

Sr. No.	RESOURCES	Exist, If Yes, How many?	If Not, please write the distance from the village in kilometre.	Any REMARKS
Sources of Irrigation				
1.	Canal			
2.	River			
3.	Shallow (Motor Pump)			
4.	Submersible			
5.	Pond			
6.	Tank			

Sr. No.	RESOURCES	Exist, If Yes, How many?	If Not, please write the distance from the village in kilometre.	Any REMARKS
7.	Trench			
8.	Ring Well			
9.	Other Irrigational Sources (Over flow)			
Machineries & Inputs				
10.	Tractor			
11.	Veterinary			
12.	Fertilizer & Pesticides Shop (Gov & Non-Gov)			
13.	Husking Machine			
Education				
14.	Pre-Primary School (Nursery)			
15.	Primary School (I-V)			
16.	Junior Basic (V-VIII)			
17.	Senior Basic (VIII-X)			
18.	Higher Secondary (X-XII)			
19.	Religious Educational Institute (Madrasa/Missionaries)			

Sr. No.	RESOURCES	Exist, If Yes, How many?	If Not, please write the distance from the village in kilometre.	Any REMARKS
20.	Adult Education Centre			
21.	College (Govt. or Non-Govt)			
22.	University			
Health & Sanitation				
23.	Health Sub-Centre			
24.	Primary Health Centre (PHC)			
25.	Sub-Divisional Hospital			
26.	District Hospital			
27.	Nursing Home			
28.	Private Allopathic Doctor			
29.	Medicine Shop			
30.	Mobile Health Unit			
31.	Life Insurance			
32.	Mutual fund			
33.	ASHA/ Health Worker			
34.	Telemedicine			

Sr. No.	RESOURCES	Exist, If Yes, How many?	If Not, please write the distance from the village in kilometre.	Any REMARKS
35.	Homeopathic Doctor			
36.	Ayurvedic Doctor			
37.	Quack Doctor			
38.	Ojha			
39.	UTBA(Untrained Birth Attendant)			
40.	TBA (Trained Birth Attendant)			
41.	Drinking Water (PHE/ Underground/Ataldhara/ RGNDWM)			
42.	I) Latrine (Pucca)			
	II) Latrine (Kuccha)			
Transportation & Communication				
43.	Post Office / Sub-post Office			
44.	Telephone/Mobile(কত			
45.	Bus Stop			
46.	Railway Station			
47.	Newspaper			

Sr. No.	RESOURCES	Exist, If Yes, How many?	If Not, please write the distance from the village in kilometre.	Any REMARKS
48.	Radio			
49.	Community TV			
50.	Cable Connection			
51.	Pucca Road			
52.	Brick / Stone Road			
53.	Kuccha Road			
54.	Internet			
Other Institutions				
55.	Market			
56.	Grocery Shop			
57.	Electricity Available			
58.	PDS			
59.	Nearest Town			
60.	District Headquarters			
61.	SDM Office			
62.	Police Station			

Sr. No.	RESOURCES	Exist, If Yes, How many?	If Not, please write the distance from the village in kilometre.	Any REMARKS
63.	High Court			
64.	Central Jail / Sub- Jail			
65.	Bio-gas			
66.	Library			
67.	Community Centre			
68.	Function Hall			
Financial Institutions				
69.	Commercial Banks like SBI, UBI, RBI etc.			
70.	Regional Banks like Gramin Bank, Coop Bank			
71.	Any Private Bank like ICICI, AXIS, etc.			
72.	Primary Agriculture Credit Society (PACS)			
73.	LAMPS			
74.	Micro-Finance Institutions			
75.	Money Lenders			
Rural Development Institutions				
76.	Self Help Groups (SHG)			

Sr. No.	RESOURCES	Exist, If Yes, How many?	If Not, please write the distance from the village in kilometre.	Any REMARKS
77.	Farmer's Club			
78.	Clubs / Voluntary Organization			
79.	Panchayat Office			
80.	Revenue Inspector Office			
81.	Block			
82.	Zila Parishad			
83.	B.L &L.R.O			
84.	ICDS			
85.	Industrial Training Institute (ITI)			
86.	NGO			
87.	Cold Storage			
88.	Total Households of the ADC / Panchayat			

DATE:

Signature of the Field Investigator

Signature of the Respondent

Bibliography

Adhikari, A. and K. Bhatia (2010), "Can we Bank on Banks?", *Economic and Political Weekly*, January 2.

Afridi, Farzana (2008), "Can Community Monitoring Improve the Accountability of Public Officials", *Economic and Political Weekly*, October 18.

Aiyar, Yamini and Salimah Samji (2006), "Improving the Effectiveness of National Rural Employment Guarantee Act", *Economic and Political Weekly*, January 28, pp. 320-326.

Aiyar, Yamini and Salimah Samji (2009), "Transparency and Accountability in NREGA: A Case Study of Andhra Pradesh", Working Paper No. 1, Accountability Initiative, Centre for Policy Research, Chanakyapuri, New Delhi, February.

Alam, S & Noor Alam, M. (2014). Governance and Employment Generation through MGNREGA. *International Journal of Economics, Commerce and Management*, Vol. II, Issue 9, Sep 2014 http://ijecm.co.uk/ ISSN 2348 038.

Ambasta, P., V. Shankar and M. Shah (2008), "Two Years of NREGA: The Road Ahead", *Economic and Political Weekly*, February 23.

Ambasta, Pramathesh, PS Vijay Shankar, Mihir Shah, 2008, "Two Years of NREGA: The Road Ahead" in *Economic and Political Weekly*, February 23.

Ambasta, Pramathesh, Vijay Shankar, P.V. and Shah, Mihir (2008) Two years of NREGA: The road ahead, *Economic and Political Weekly*, 43 (8): 41-50.

Anderson, Siwan, Ashok Kotwal, Ashwini Kulkarni and Bharat Ramaswami (2013), "Measuring the Impacts of Linking NREGA Payments to UID", Working Paper, International Growth Centre, London School of Economics and Political Science, London.

B.K. Parate, Harshad, Verma, Murari, Malaviya, Sumedha, Rao, Ananya S. Sengupta, Asmita, Kattumuri, Ruth and Ravindranath, N.H. (2011) MGNREGA for environmental service enhancement and vulnerability reduction: Rapid appraisal in Chitradurga district, Karnataka, *Economic and Political Weekly*, 66 (20): 39-47.

Bardhan, Kalpana (2011) Rural employment, wages and labour markets in India: A survey of research-III, *Economic and Political Weekly*, 12 (28): 1101-1118.

Bhowmik, I & Bose, Pritam (2015). Efficiency and Impact of MGNREGS in Tripura. *Social Change and Development*, Vol. XII No.1, 2015.

Bhowmik, I (2013). MGNREGA in Tripura: A Study of Efficiency and Equity. www.researchgate.net/publications/264310095 DOI: 10.13140/2.1.1067.3604

CAG (2008), "Performance Audit of Implementation of National Rural Employment Guarantee Act", Report No. 11, Comptroller and Auditor General of India, Government of India.

Chakraborty, Pinaki (2007), "Implementation of Employment Guarantee: A Preliminary Apprisal", *Economic and Political Weekly*, February 17, pp. 548-551.

Chambers, R. and Conway G, R. (1992), "Sustainable Rural Livelihoods: Practical Concepts for the 21st Century", *Institute of Development Studies (IDS) Discussion Paper 296.*

Chatterjee, R., Mukherjee, D. and Deb, A. (2018), "A Study on Factors Responsible for Growth of Entrepreneurship in North East India with Special Reference to Tripura", *Optimization: Journal of Management*, Vol.10, Issue 1.

Costantini,V & Monni, S(2007): Environment, Human Development, and Economic Growth; Ecological Economics : A Trans disciplinary, *Journal on Ecological Economics* JEL classification: Q15; Q01; Q56 ; doi:10.1016/j.ecolecon.2007.05.011 www.elselvier.com.

Debnath N. & Neogi D, (2013). "A Study on the Impact of Mahatma Gandhi National Rural Employment Guarantee Act (MGNREGA) on Generation and Distribution of Sustainable Assets among Tribal and Non-Tribal Population in Tripura State of North-East India". *International Journal of Advanced Research* (2013), Volume 1, Issue 8, 711-721.

Dreze, Jean, Nikhil Dev and Reetika Khera (2008), "Corruption in NREGA: Myths and Reality", *The Hindu* dated 22 January.

Farrington, J. (2007), "Sustainable Livelihoods, Rights and the New Architecture of Aid", *Natural Resource Perspectives*, 2007.

Gaur, A. (1985), "*Integrated Rural Area Development: A Case Study of a Tahsil*", B.R Publishing Corporation, Delhi.

Ghosh, J., (2009) Equity and Inclusion through Public Expenditure: The potential of the NREGS. Paper presented at the International Conference on NREGA, Ministry of Rural Development and ICAR. [Online]. Available:www.macroscan.com/pol/jan09/pdf/NREGS.pdf on [18.05.2020& 15.09.2020]

Gupta, S.K, Fearooz Ahmad, Asset Creation under MGNREGA (2015), Volume 5, Issue 1, IJMIE

Haberfeld, Y., Menaria, R.K., Sahoo, B. B. and Vyas R. N. (2011) Seasonal migration of rural labor in India, *Population Research and Policy Review*, 18 (5): 473-489.

Harrison, Fidel Ezeala (2011) Analysis of wage formation processes in rural agriculture, *The Journal of Developing Areas*, 38 (1): 79-92.

Hirway, Indira, 2006 "Globalization, Labour Markets and Gender Inequity: Consultant on India Study", prepared for UNOPS (United Nations Office for Project Services).

India Village Directory@Vlist.in accessed online on 27.11.2020.

International Bank for Reconstruction and Development/The World Bank (2016): *Bhutan's Labor Market : Toward Gainful Quality Employment for All.*

International Labour Office (ILO), *Global Wage Report*, 2009.

Jacob, Naomi (2008), "The Impact of NREGA on Rural-Urban Migration: Field survey of Villupuram District, Tamil Nadu", CCS Working Paper No. 202, Summer Research Internship Programme, Centre for Civil Society.

Jenkins, Stephens, P and John Mickleweight eds., 2007, *Inequality and Poverty Reexamined*, Oxford University Press, New York.

Jha, Raghbendra, Raghav, Gaiha, Shyalshri, Shankar, 2008, "Reviewing the National Rural Employment Guarantee Programme", in *Economic and Political Weekly*, March 15, pp. 44- 48.

Kareemulla, K., S. Kumar, K.S. Reddy, C.A. Rama Rao and B. Venketeswarlu (2010), "Impact of NREGS on Rural Livelihoods and Agricultural Capital Formation", *Indian Journal of Agricultural Economics*, Vol. 65 No. 3, pp. 524-539.

Keerthi, K.,Bhattarai, M., Kamala, T.S. and Rao, P.P. (2014), "MGNREGA Impact on Rural Asset Creation: a study in two villages of Prakasam District of Andhra Pradesh, India", Presented in an International Seminar on "*Flagship Programmes: Impact, Problems & Challenges Ahead*", 19-21 November 2014, National Institute of Rural Development (NIRD) Hyderabad.

Keynes, J. M. (1977). *The General Theory of Employment, Interest and Money*, The Macmillan Press, London.

Khera, Reetika (2008), "Employment Guarantee Act", *Economic and Political Weekly*, August 30, pp. 8-10.

Khera, Reetika and Nayak, Nandini (2009) Women workers and perceptions of rural Employment Guarantee Act, *Economic and Political Weekly*, 64 (43): 49-57.

Kumar, A, Ambasta P, Arya V, Panda B, Narayan S, Kesavan P.K, Singh S.K & Badrinarayan. (2010): *Working Group Report On Capacity Building, Volume 1: Main Report;* Central Employment Guarantee Council.

Kumar, D.M, Kabir, Y & James, A.J (2016). *Rural Water Systems for Multiple Uses and Livelihood Security*. Imprint: Elselveir. Published on May 2016.

Laurent, Eloi, 2007, "Globalization: End of the Beginning or Beginning of the End" in *The Globalist*, www.theglobalist.com

Liu, Yanyan and Christopher B. Barrett (2013), "Heterogeneous Pro Poor Targeting in National Rural Employment Guarantee Scheme", *Economic and Political Weekly*, Vol. XLVIII, No. 10, March 9, pp. 46-53.

Mehrotra, Santosh, 2008, "NREG Two Years on : Where Do We Go from Here? *Economic and Political Weekly*, August 2, pp 27-35.

Ministry of Rural Development, 2008b NREGA Operational Guidelines, Delhi: Government of India.

Mishra, S. K, (2010), "Asset Creation under MGNREGA: A Study in Three Districts of Madhya Pradesh", *IMJ*, Volume 3 Issue 3.

Mukherjee, D. Chatterjee, R., and Deb, A. (2018), "A Study on Factors Responsible for Growth of Entrepreneurship in North East India with Special Reference to Tripura", *Optimization: Journal of Management*, Vol.10, Issue 1.

Mukherjee, D., Chatterjee, R., Chakraborty G, Deb A., (2017) Factors Influencing Growth of Rural Entrepreneurship in Tripura A Socio-Economic Perspective, *Manthan –The Journal of Innovations*, Vol. XII.1, Jan-June 2017. p. 47-57, ISSN: 0976-1713. Indexed by Ulrich. UGC's List of Journals Sl. no. 6673.

Mukherjee, D., Chatterjee, R., (2019) *An Empirical Study on Livelihood Challenges of Old Age Persons of Tripura with Special Reference to Tribal Population, Development & Tribes: Contemporary Issues & Challenges* (Eds.), Serials Publications (P) Ltd., New Delhi, p. 415-437, ISBN 9789386611635.

Mukherjee D, Chatterjee R, Mitra S (2020) MGNREGA on People's Health and Quality of Life: Opening of a Novel Market for Health, Purvottaran – The Rise of North East: Paradigms of Development in the VUCA World (Ed.), Bloomsbury Publication, ISBN: 9789390513017, p 111-122.

Narayana, N.S.S, Parikh S.K. and Srinivasan T.N(1991): *Agriculture, Growth, and Redistribution of Income: Policy Analysis with a General Equilibrium Model of India;* edited Volume 190, p. 1-301.

Nathan, Dev, D Narasimha Reddy, and Govind Kelkar, 2008, International Trade and Global Civil Society, Routledge, New Delhi.

Pellisary, S and Jalan S.K. (2011). Towards transformative social protection: a gendered analysis of the Employment Guarantee Act of India (MGNREGA). *Journal of Gender & Development*, Vol.19, 2011, Issue 2: Social Protection. https://doi.org/10.1080/13552074.2011.592639

Priya (1998), "Role of Panchayati Raj in Implementation of NREGA", National Study Phase III, New Delhi.

Raju, V.T. (2011) The impact of new farm technology on human labour employment, *Indian Journal of Industrial Relations*, 11(4): 439-510.

Rawls, John. (1971), *"A Theory of Justice"*, The Belknap Press of Harvard University Press.

Rogaly, Ben (2011) Workers on the move: Seasonal migration and changing social relations in rural India, *Gender and Development*, 6 (1): 21-29.

Roy, S (2010). Implementation of NREGS in Tripura: An Evaluation. *The NEHU Journal*, Vol. VIII, No. 1, January 2010.

Sankaran, Kamala (2011) NREGA wages: Ensuring decent work, *Economic and Political Weekly*, 66 (7): 23-25.

Scoones, I. (1998), "Sustainable Rural Livelihoods: A framework for analysis", Institute of Development Studies Working Paper 72. University of Sussex: Brighton.

Shah, M. (2009), "Taking goals of NREGA-I forward", *The Hindu,* 14 August.

Shah, Mihir (2007) Employment guarantee, civil society and Indian democracy, *Economic and Political Weekly*, 42(45 & 46): 43-51.

Shome et al (2012). Impact of Workfare Programmes on Quality of Life: A Case Study of National Rural Employment Guarantee Act in India. *Stirling International Journal of Postgraduate Research* 1.1 (2012).

Sultana, M & Rao, K.T (2016). Socio-Economic Development Through Indian Government Scheme –MGNREGA: A Review on West Bengal *State: International Journal on Approximate Reasoning*; DOI 10.21474/IJAR01/1470 Corpus ID:1251.

Sundaram, K., 2007, "Employment and Poverty in India, 2000-2005," in *Economic and Political Weekly*, July 28: 3121-3131.

The Economic Times (2020), March 2020.

The Economic Times, March 2017 accessed online on 18.09.2020.

Ujjawal A, Champatiray, A. K, Sadhu, S and Mendiratta, T. (2010). *Business Correspondent Model: An Analysis the Financial Viability of Customer Service Providers and Client Satisfaction.* IFMR Research, Centre for Micro Finance, Bankers Institute of Rural Development (BIRD).

Ujjawal A., Champatiray, A K., Sadhu, S., and Mendiratta, T. (2010), "*Business Correspondent Model: An Analysis the Financial Viability of Customer Service Providers and Client Satisfaction*", IFMR Research, Centre for Micro Finance, Bankers Institute of Rural Development (BIRD).

Vij, N (2011). Collaborative Governance – Analysing Social Audits in MGNREGA. *IDS Bulletin* Volume 42 Number 6 November 2011. Institute of Development Studies. Pp 28,32.

World Food Programme-Supported Pond Development Project in Central Rakhine State: *Asset Creation & Livelihoods*, WFP Myanmar, 2019.

Zaman, H. (2016). Assessing the Impact of Employment Generation Programs in Challenging Rural Poverty: A Comparative Study on Bangladesh and India. *Journal of Poverty,* July 2011. DOI: 10.1080/10875549.2011.588303

Zorlu, Aslan and Hartog, Joop (2003). The effect of immigration on wages in three European countries, *Journal of Population Economics*, 18 (1): 113-151.

Web Reference

http://data.worldbank.org/indicator/SP.RUR.TOTL.ZS?year_high_desc=false

www.ecostat.gov.in. accessed online on 27.11.2020.

Index

About the Authors

Prof. Debarshi Mukherjee is an alumnus of Visva Bharati, Santiniketan, and Banasthali Vidyapith, Rajasthan. Currently, he is a Professor and Head of the Department of Business Management, Tripura University. He has established the state's first business incubator fully funded by the Ministry of MSME, Govt. of India. Having specialized in the information systems domain, his research interest lies in developing blended learning models and ICT intervention in tertiary education, ensuring learning continuity. Besides teaching and academic administration, he has worked extensively in Curricula Design and Innovative Andragogy Development over the last two decades. His endeavor in research has earned him over 100 publications to his credit. He has worked in many funded projects sponsored by NABARD and ICSSR. He has delivered over 100 invited talks and chaired technical sessions at many conclaves. He has also deliberated in the different television/radio shows in Tripura and Bangladesh. He writes regularly for newspapers and news portals on contemporary issues.

He has recently published an edited volume titled Purvottaran– The Rise of Northeast: Paradigms of Development in the VUCA World was published by Bloomsbury, and the foreword was written by the Hon'ble Chief Minister, Govt. of Tripura.

Dr. Rajesh Chatterjee (b 1973) is a Rural Development professional and achieved M.A & Ph.D. in Rural Development from the Department of Rural Reconstruction & Development, Visva-Bharati. He has earned 15 years' experience in Academic and Action Research and worked at several organisations and the Department of Rural Development, Visva-Bharati as Project Associate. Presently he is engaged as Assistant Professor, Tribal Studies (CSSEIP),

Tripura University, Tripura. He handled the projects of UGC, Save the Children-UK, NRHM, JICA, DEAR-NABARD, ICSSR, IIDS-UNICEF, IIPA-New Delhi, ONGC-CSR, MTA-GoI, SSA-GoT, ITTO, TRPC-GoT, TFDPC-GoT and also worked as a consultant of various organisations. He is an expert of Project Management, Extension work, PRA/PLA. He attended several National and International Seminars & published several articles in national and international journals, and published books.

Sudakhina Mitra is a Research Scholar in the Department of Business Management, Tripura University, and faculty in the Administrative Training Institute of the State of Tripura, commonly known as the State Institute of Public Administration and Rural Development (SIPARD). She is an MPhil in Health Economics from Jadavpur University, Kolkata, West Bengal. She has worked as a project fellow in the Planning & Development Unit of the Department of Economics, Jadavpur University. Her major publications include "Conflict, Displacement and Inequality of Opportunity"-Asian Journal of Peace Building Vol. 4 No. 2 (2016): 137-59; "Pattern of Public Health Care and Health System Infrastructure"- Social Science Research Network. SSRN: https://ssrn.com/abstract=2783275 or http://dx.doi.org/10.2139/ssrn.2783275 and "MGNREGA on People's Health & Quality Of Life - Opening of a Novel Market For Health"- Book Chapter in Purvottaran: The Rise of North East: Paradigms of Development in VUCA World.